Index on Censorship

Free Word Centre, 60 Farringdon Road, London, ECIR 3GA

Chief Executive John Kampfner **Editor** Jo Glanville **Associate Editor** Rohan Jayasekera **Assistant Editor** Natasha Schmidt **News Editor** Padraig Reidy **Online Editor** Emily Butselaar **Programme Manager, Arts and Youth** Julia Farrington **Head of Events** Sara Rhodes **Finance Manager** David Sewell **Head of Advocacy** Michael Harris **Head of Development** Lizzie Rusbridger **Events Assistant** Eve Jackson **US Editor** Emily Badger **US Head of Development** Bridget Gallagher **Editorial Assistant** Sara Yasin **Interns** Merna Azzeh, Olga Birukova, Rebecca Chao, Marta Cooper, Sarah Cox, Laura MacPhee
Graphic designer Sam Hails
Cover design Brett Biedscheid
Printed by Page Bros., Norwich, UK

Volume 40 No 3 2011

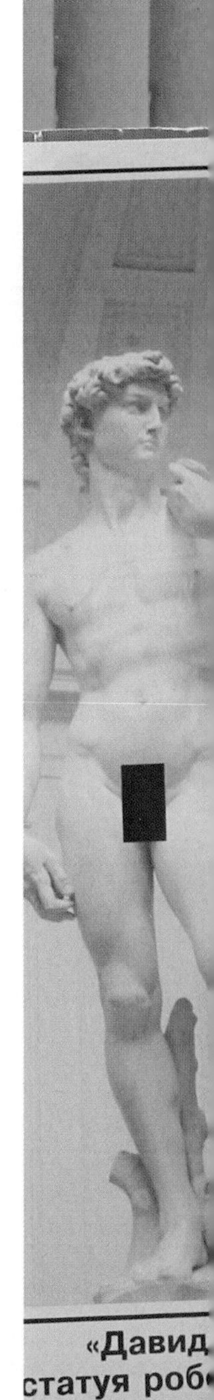

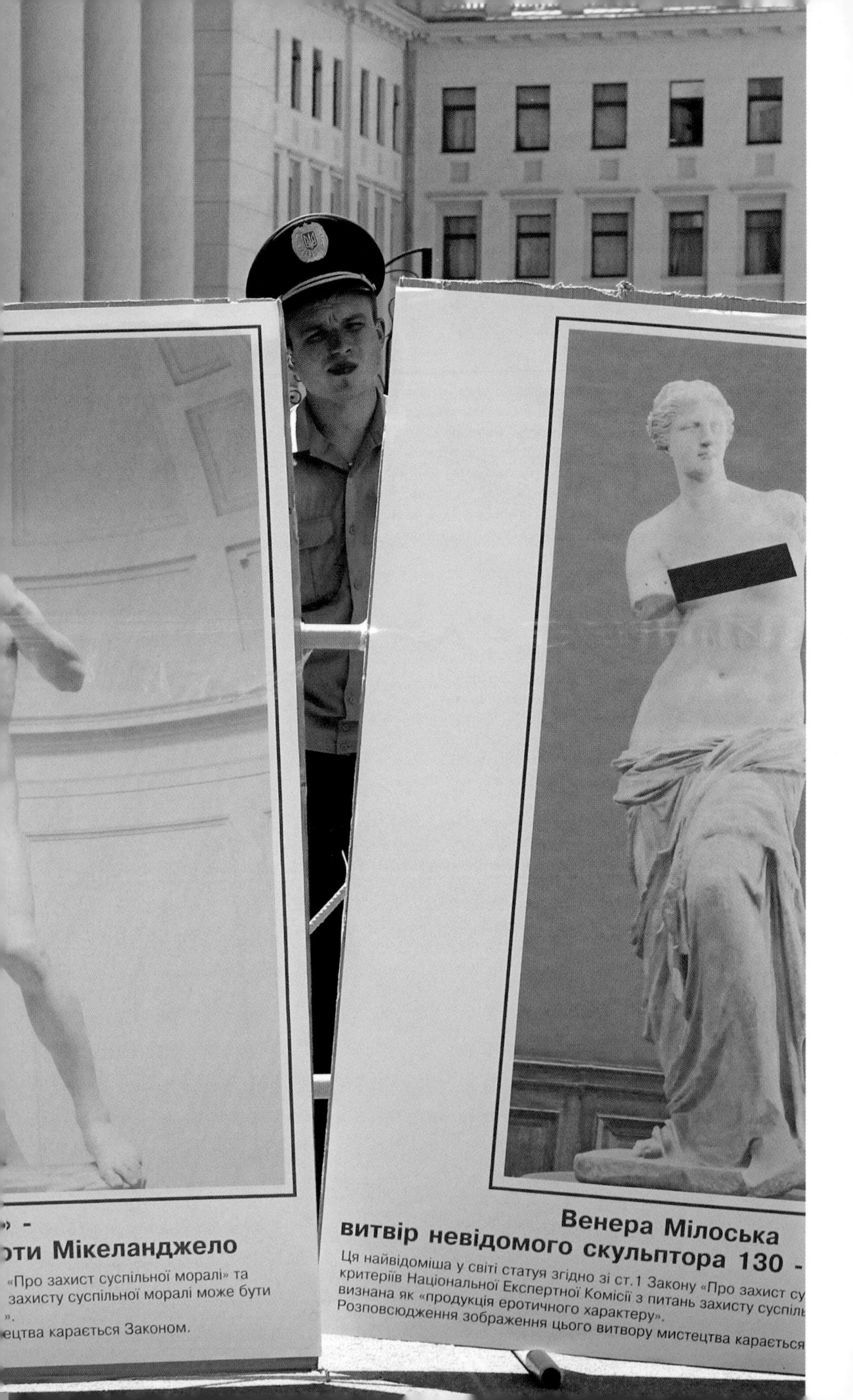

» -
оти Мікеланджело
«Про захист суспільної моралі» та
захисту суспільної моралі може бути
».
ецтва карається Законом.
Венера Мілоська
витвір невідомого скульптора 130 -
Ця найвідоміша у світі статуя згідно зі ст.1 Закону «Про захист су
критеріїв Національної Експертної Комісії з питань захисту суспіль
визнана як «продукція еротичного характеру».
Розповсюдження зображення цього витвору мистецтва карається

LIMITS OF FREEDOM

Jo Glanville

The defence of artistic expression took several paces backwards last year in the US, when the Smithsonian in Washington bowed to conservative pressure and removed a video installation by the late artist David Wojnarowicz which had been denounced as anti-Catholic. As *Washington Post* art critic Philip Kennicott observes in a perceptive essay on the debacle, it marked the first notable case of censorship since the 90s. The decision to ban the work, he notes with concern, will make all galleries now vulnerable to censorship in the name of offence, undoing the valuable progress over the past decade that has created a more permissive climate for artists in the US. It is in their inconsistent response in the defence of art, more than in any other field of creative expression, that democracies most frequently show the limits of their support for the right to freedom of expression. When it comes to sex, religion and the forces of conservatism, there can be worryingly little to separate the supposedly free society from the repressive regime. In Sharjah, in the United Arab Emirates, the director of the Biennial lost his job this year after exception was taken to Mustapha Benfodil's installation, which included text about a rape by Islamic militants (pp. 155-168); in Lebanon, a humorous image by celebrated Iranian artist Parastou Forouhar was censored for fear of causing religious offence (pp. 34-37); in London, galleries may call in the lawyers to vet shows before they open to forestall trouble – photographs of naked children, even by acclaimed photographers whose work is well known, may result in a visit from the police.

Every artist and gallery has to negotiate the degree of freedom society will allow them. As Kennicott observes, in order to display art that may shock or upset an audience, and protect their public funding, galleries are careful to underline their role as educational and social institutions, and the importance of maintaining an open space for a range of expression. Compare that balancing act with the experiences of the esteemed artist and gallery owner Rozita Sharafjahan (pp. 118-125), who runs a leading gallery in Tehran for

Protest in Kiev, Ukraine, 15 June 2011. Under new 'morality' laws, demonstrators claim that many works of art will be criminalised
Credit: Gleb Garanich/Reuters

Artists
Space

38 Greene Street
3rd Floor
New York
NY 10013
T 212 226 3970
www.artistsspace.org

contemporary art. Although she challenges the status quo with her shows (including an installation last year that daringly transformed the gallery into a presidential campaign centre for the former candidate Mir Hossein Moussavi), art is kept entirely outside the wider public space. So however audacious the shows on display in her gallery, their impact is limited. In Russia, at the other extreme, the performance artists Voina, described as 'art terrorists' by their admirer Banksy, mock the authorities and the law with their provocative actions (pp. 89-102); it is no coincidence that the state hits back against Voina with the same laws that it uses against political activists.

When Anish Kapoor withdrew from participation in the 'UK Now' festival, due to take place in China next year and organised by the British Council, in protest at the arrest of Ai Weiwei earlier this year, he threw down the gauntlet to the artistic community. ' I think it's essential that while there are still a hundred and more intellectuals locked up in Chinese jails it's the duty of all artists to stand up and say we won't take part,' Anish Kapoor tells *Index in Censorship* in an exclusive interview (pp. 14-19). 'I called out to artists all over – don't take part, don't show in China.' It's a stand that challenges the British Council's position on engaging with repressive regimes: 'It is through cultural exchange that we best demonstrate the benefits of free artistic expression and build supportive links between people in the UK and China,' its chief executive Martin Davidson said in support of the China festival. Kapoor rejects the argument; he has challenged the British Council to dedicate the central piece of the show to Ai Weiwei. 'The governmental view of the past 30 years has been we'll speak quietly in public and loudly in private,' he says. 'Well, 30 years of doing that hasn't done a damn thing … silence says there are economic interests that override human rights interests.'

We'd like to thank the BBC World Service Trust for making it possible to publish *Index on Censorship* in colour for the first time in the magazine's history. ❐

40(3): 1/5
DOI 10.1177/0306422011419469
www.indexoncensorship.org

CONTENTS

TIMELINE

INDEX INDEX

'The block project' by the Blue Noses group, Marat Gelman Gallery, Moscow, January 2005
Credit: Dmitry Korobeinikov/RIA Novosti

THE ART ISSUE

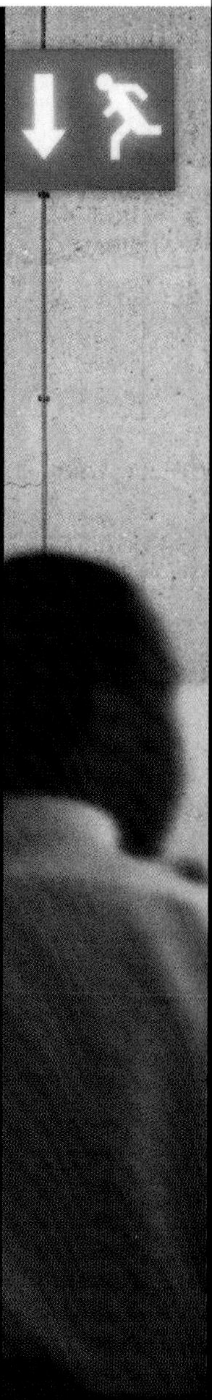

Credit: Brett Biedscheid

Ai Weiwei: 'Marble Chair', 2008, marble, 120 × 56 × 46 cm
Courtesy: Ai Weiwei and Lisson Gallery

A SINGULAR VOICE

Anish Kapoor explains why artists have a duty to take a political stand for freedom of expression

Celebrated sculptor Anish Kapoor campaigned for Ai Weiwei's release this year, when he was detained for 81 days, and withdrew as a protest from participation in the British Council 'UK Now' show next year in China.

Index: When you made the decision to withdraw from the show in Beijing and to make a stand for Ai Weiwei, had you ever made that kind of political gesture before?

Anish Kapoor: When Ai Weiwei was arrested, I was doing this work in Paris at the Grand Palais ['Leviathan']. I thought about it long and hard – should I, shouldn't I dedicate the work to Ai Weiwei? What does it mean? One has to be very clear that in doing such a thing you never do it without a degree of self-interest. I needed to understand what my self-interest was and what I was trying to do. Was this about Ai Weiwei or was it about me? And I decided in the end that as one of the big shows in Europe during the summer, I could dedicate it to Ai Weiwei and that it wasn't about me. I discovered in doing it that actually I have a voice that I probably didn't know I had before and I think that's very important. And then I felt that since I'd already taken a stand, the show that the British Council was planning ['UK Now' in China next year] required a further stand. I think it's essential that while there are still a hundred and more people locked up in Chinese jails – I'm talking about intellectuals, I'm not for the moment talking about ordinary people who go on the internet – I think it's the duty of all artists to stand up and say we won't take part. I've called out to artists all over – don't take part, don't show in China. A few have started to respond. I see that Daniel Buren, the great French conceptual artist, has pulled a show in China, and there are others. I'm glad to see it. It means something.

Index: You also proposed that galleries close for a day across the world and said it would be good for the art world to come together more.

Anish Kapoor: It's perhaps naïve of me, but I think it's important that we stand together for colleagues. It's very hard for galleries to close for a day, but rather than a negative action, I feel in the end we were about to make a positive action on the anniversary of the 100 days of Ai Weiwei's incarceration, but thankfully he was released. The positive action was to try and get thousands of galleries all over the world to show a work of Ai Weiwei's.

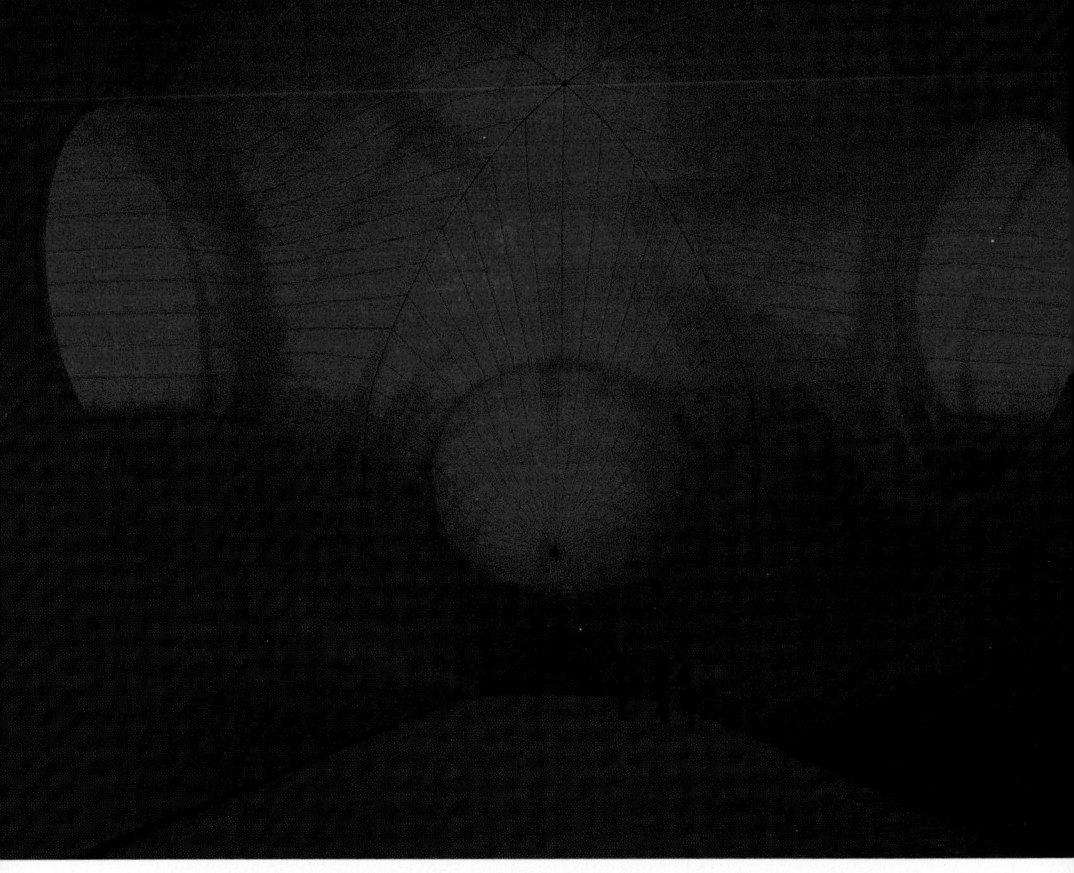

Anish Kapoor: 'Leviathan', 2001, PVC, 33.6 × 99.89 × 72.23m, Monumenta 2011, Grand Palais, Paris
Photo: Dave Morgan/Courtesy the artist

Index: China is an extreme case in the degree to which it controls, and attempts to control, freedom of expression. Would you like to see the art world being more politically engaged and showing more solidarity? There's a very long tradition of writers coming together, but not in the art world.

Anish Kapoor: The art world is extremely fragmented. It is a place that's also infiltrated by money and other instruments of influence. And it never finds itself in a place where it can shout. I think we need to learn how to do that and find a way to have singular voices. Through the whole period of Soviet repression of artists, which was severe, the art world didn't say a thing. The avant-garde has held itself away from human rights. It's been a great struggle for artists of non-European origin. It's been a great struggle for women artists, quite contrary to the sense that the aesthetic world is an open forum – it isn't. It's extremely doctrinaire and extremely partisan. And I think those battles are still being fought. So it's not surprising at one level anyway.

I can only explain it by [the fact that] these old instruments of power in the art world are generally male and white, and within a certain aesthetic tradition. All of that has begun to fall apart in the last decade or so. We still haven't got to the point where, if you like, lone, outsider voices can be properly heard. Ai Weiwei is a celebrity, so it's relatively easy [for him to be heard] – much harder in many other cases.

Index: Artists are more subject to arbitrary censorship wherever they are – whether in the free world or more repressive world.

Anish Kapoor: I think it's also because contemporary visual culture isn't unidirectional. When you write a piece, you have to articulate a precise point in words – political or otherwise. An art work can be nebulous in relation to the politics of its situation. It can indicate a discomfort without actually articulating it and therefore it's much harder to pin down. It's much harder to say: 'This is subversive.' It's hard to define what subversive is – especially in contemporary language and contemporary visual culture. Ai Weiwei, in that sense, is somewhat more articulated towards a series of events – noting down the number of people killed by corruption and maladministration, or collecting and making monuments with marbled doors of all the houses that have been knocked down and land that's been taken away from the so-called squatters. It's still nebulous though. If you look at the work it's just a bunch of marbled doors. It doesn't obviously say what we infer from it. Though we know what to infer of course.

Index: I'm also thinking of artists in the West. There's a famous case of the Smithsonian last year bowing to conservative pressure. There's galleries in London that have problems when they show the work of Sally Mann for example.

Anish Kapoor: I think we have a very carefully defined sense of what's acceptable, especially if it goes near children or pornography – all those much more difficult areas. Censorship is there and some of it is okay, I assume. But how we monitor it is important.

Index: When you say it's ok ...

Anish Kapoor: I can see that there's a reason to monitor pornography and paedophilia, especially unacceptable things, and we have to understand that anything that encourages them has to be watched carefully. I understand that impulse but we go there, even there, with great care.

Index: Artists are by the very nature of their work going to be more vulnerable to pressures of conservatism or conformism.

Anish Kapoor: Of course. There's a kind of naughty boy or naughty girl way of doing it which a lot of artists have taken – why not? I'm not that kind of artist at all. I feel that agitprop as a method is problematic – for me – in terms of my poetic understanding of what a work can be.

Index: I wanted to ask you about the British Council's response to the dilemma of artists displaying work in countries that have a poor human rights record. Chief executive Martin Davidson has said: 'It is through cultural exchange that we best demonstrate the benefits of free artistic expression and build supportive links between people in the UK and China.'

Anish Kapoor: I say phooey to that I'm afraid. I did suggest to them [that they] ought to make the central piece in the [UK Now] show a kind of dedication to Ai Weiwei – or to one of the other artists. If they're going to do this show then they ought to have [Chinese] artists properly take part. The governmental view over the past 30 years has been we'll speak quietly in public and loudly in private. Well, 30 years of doing that hasn't done a damn thing. We had the premier of China here [in London] and [David] Cameron was silent on the subject. [Was that] just because Ai was released? No, that was carefully timed. And I think silence says that there are economic interests that override human rights interests. It's disgraceful.

Index on Censorship: China's one of the most flagrant examples [of human rights abuse], Iran would be another. Would you start applying the same [tactics] to other countries?

Anish Kapoor: One has to. In the end one has to. Iranian culture, like Chinese culture, is extraordinary. One has to take a moral stand in a way with colleagues for solidarity. I think it's important to understand in this also that governments are ineffective. I think that's maybe the most important point of all. Individuals have to do it all. So therefore it's our duty as individuals to stand up and say we won't take part or protest. The Chinese don't listen to anyone while there are government protests – I have absolutely no doubt whatsoever that it's individuals making a noise all over the world that made them release Ai Weiwei. I've no doubt about it. Governments are just ineffective at this. And we have the power. We must do something. ❐

Anish Kapoor was talking to Jo Glanville

40(3): 14/19
DOI 10.1177/0306422011419608
www.indexoncensorship.org

CHINA'S NEW DEAL

The artist Ai Weiwei's outspoken views are gaining currency. **Simon Kirby** reflects on a change of mood in China as people lose faith in the Party

In June, Ai Weiwei was released from his recent detention to a form of home surveillance. He is confined to the city of Beijing and must inform the authorities of his movements. He may not make public statements nor comment on his detention and the terms of his release (a condition he has already breached); further investigations are pending and a prosecution may be pursued within a year. It is still far from clear what the implications are for Ai as a private individual, let alone for his capacity to continue to work as an artist. Just as he was never formally arrested neither has he been fully freed.

This shabby story takes place against a backdrop of heightened political sensitivity in China as the country braces itself for transition to a new, as yet unannounced, group of top leaders. This is scheduled to take place next year in the Great Hall of the People during the 18th National Congress of the Communist Party. The Congress will certainly be a rigid spectacle of national purpose and will make numbing television viewing. Not least because it will be impossible not to speculate on the nature of the Byzantine succession struggle which is currently taking place behind firmly locked doors.

Ai Weiwei: 'Surveillance Camera', 2006, marble
Courtesy: Lisson Gallery/the artist

Ai Weiwei's social activism, such as his support for the prosecuted journalists investigating the collapse of schools during the 2008 Sichuan earthquake, has been widely reported in the West but received little coverage in the Chinese state media. Nevertheless, his influential blog, closed down in 2009, had been avidly followed in many circles in China, including amongst his fellow artists. Certain groups of people witnessed his provocative stance with quiet admiration and bated breath. A more common response, however, has been impatience with his provocation of the government and the view that he had courted trouble. He has been criticised for being a self-publicist with little concern for the well-being of his more vulnerable supporters. There are also detractors overseas who have seen him, at best, as a member of the privileged elite who pander directly to the western media and, at worst, as a Communist Party stooge.

> Artists were co-opted with sticks and carrots. There were rewards to be had

The detention of Ai Weiwei was based on intimidation rather than legal process – a pattern that is well established in China. In effect, he was kidnapped by the state and never informed which organ of the machinery was holding him, nor was he charged with a specific crime. Rather, his indictment was based on 'confessions'. Even his release was justified on the spurious grounds of cooperative behaviour, willingness to make amends and poor physical health. As the threat of re-opening the case against him still looms, he is now being blackmailed into falling into line.

A few weeks after Ai Weiwei was released I had lunch with him. He talked frankly about the contradictions of his detention and the absurdity of his current position. He clearly intends to continue working and his remarkable personal charisma is undimmed. Yet he is, in my view, a person who is also deeply disturbed by what is happening to him.

Throughout the 90s, Chinese state-controlled capitalism ushered in a remarkable economic boom from which the fledgling contemporary art scene benefited. Artists, as potentially problematic figures, were heavily co-opted with a variety of sticks and carrots – there were rich rewards to be had and the freedom to continue making, exhibiting and travelling was

Ai Weiwei: 'Coloured Vases', 2010, 31 Han Dynasty vases and industrial paint
Courtesy: Lisson Gallery/the artist

granted to artists in exchange for creating non-critical work. In many cases, artists were understandably tempted to comply. Ever since the fearful events of the Tiananmen massacre on 4 June 1989, there has been an enforced accommodation between the government and society. I dubbed this the 'Tiananmen contract' in an article for *Index on Censorship* that was published in 2008, ahead of the Chinese Olympics. The deal is that the Communist Party would steer the people towards individual prosperity and the country to greatness, through ensuring stability. In return, the primacy of the Party could never be questioned. Three years ago, the contract was widely supported – the level of basic freedom was greater than it had been in 20 years and living standards were rising. There was also pride at China's leading role on the world stage. Today, I believe this consensus is much more fragile.

The daily reality for Chinese citizens is that living costs are rising fast and incomes are not keeping up. Working conditions for white collar workers

(continues on p.30)

Song Dong and Yin Xiuzhen: an elegy for the disappeared

Husband and wife Song Dong and Yin Xiuzhen are among the two most widely internationally exhibited artists on the Chinese contemporary art scene. This year they opened an exhibition in Beijing which is a continuation of an occasional ten-year collaboration which explores their lives together as artists, as a couple and as parents to an adored young daughter.

The theme of the collaboration is simply the quotidian 'chopstick'. One chopstick being perfectly useless without its pair, this acts as a metaphor of mutual interdependence and cooperation in daily life. *Chopsticks III*, the latest work in this collaboration, is a large sculptural installation that literally represents a pair of chopsticks that disassembles into sections – one section of Song's pairs with one of Yin's.

Yin Xiuzhen's yellow steel chopstick references the arm of the ubiquitous crane – the tool for the destruction of the old city neighbourhoods and the dramatic creation of a new and alienating high-rise city. Thousands of frayed garment fragments, a signature material for the artist, are clamped tightly into the length of the metal struts and refer, with a certain quiet poetry, to the many millions of individual lives coerced into the mass modernisation project of the new Chinese city.

Song Dong's red wooden chopstick references the pillar and roof beam of traditional Beijing domestic architecture which has been almost completely erased. His disassembled sections containing miniaturised, mirrored scenarios are part nostalgic references to individual domestic life of 1980s China among the symbols of an authoritarian capital.

At the same time, this sequence offers a poignant and deserted narrative of the fateful days leading up to the Tiananmen massacre of 4 June 1989. One section shows a miniature red-coloured profile of the great buildings that surround the square, another shows a meeting hall typical of government buildings, a third shows the white markings of an empty night-time road. A deserted Chang

An Boulevard, down which the tanks rolled to enter Tiananmen, is shown with its characteristic eastern bloc decorative street lamps and central lane barriers. Another piece represents a couple of loud hailers like those used to warn the students to vacate the squatted square. Most explicitly of all, the rounded end-section of Song's red chopstick is called simply 'Bullet'. When one peers into the mirrored section 'Kaleidoscope', one sees one's own fractured face splashed with blood-red paint.

Poignantly, the remaining sections refer simply to elements of daily life – miniature wooden bed frames typical of the student dormitory and the once ubiquitous mini cooking stove that burns cheap coal briquettes. Even Song's signature video sequence of slicing vegetables becomes somehow sinister as the big chopper continues to slice the vegetables into a kind of useless vegetable mince.

A middle section of 'Chopsticks III' is called 'Seal' and represents the ubiquitous Chinese business chop that is needed to make any agreement official. This is the Chinese government's deal with its people.

Song and Yin refer, albeit gently, to the violence done through authoritarian means to Chinese citizens in the process of modernising their economy and their city. To depict the events of 4 June is strictly disallowed in China and it is a tribute to the artists that they managed to do so publicly, but with such discretion that it passed under the radar of the official censors. It is also significant that they evoked a haunting memory of those events, officially erased and suppressed, just at the time when the deal that Tiananmen created is under such widespread questioning and scrutiny. *Simon Kirby*

Captions

Page 26: *Song Dong & Yin Xiuzhen: 'Chopsticks III, Avenue', 2011, detail*
Courtesy: the artists/Chambers Fine Art

Page 27: *Song Dong & Yin Xiuzhen: 'Chopsticks III, Seal', detail and 'Chopsticks III', 2011*
Courtesy: the artists/Chambers Fine Art

Page 28: *Song Dong & Yin Xiuzhen: 'Chopsticks III, Bed Roll', detail, 2011*
Courtesy: the artists/Chambers Fine Art

Page 29: *Song Dong & Yin Xiuzhen: 'Chopsticks III, Crane arm', detail, 2011*
Courtesy: the artists/Chambers Fine Art

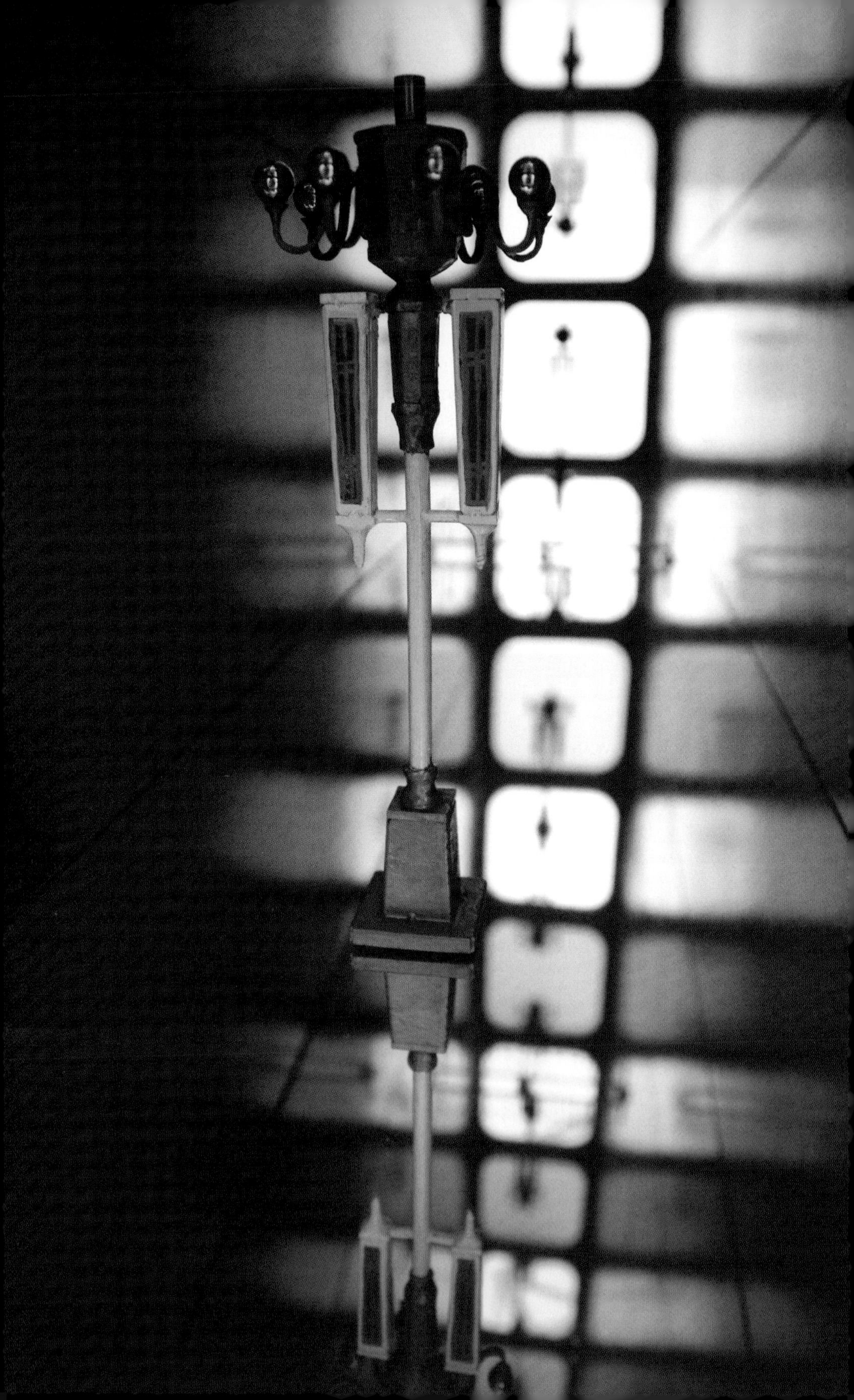

(continued from p.23)
can be demoralising, while those for migrant manual workers, who continue to have even basic rights denied them, are often shockingly exploitative. Commuting in the new, high-rise cities can be exhausting and alienating. People are deeply sceptical about the capacity of the state to protect them from (often deliberately) contaminated food and a toxic living environment, criminal scams, corruption in the medical profession and corporate exploitation of consumers. The Party is widely understood to be at the centre of many of these scandals and is often seen to be protecting wrongdoers. Most flagrantly, the new super-rich live effectively beyond the reach of the law, while ordinary people can in no way count on basic social justice for themselves and their families.

There are attempts to address these problems through draconian anti-corruption campaigns which make examples of officials accused of vice and graft. There are also strenuous efforts to reform social and fiscal legislation and to professionalise the legal system. This year's 90th anniversary celebrations of the founding of the Chinese Communist Party saw an outpouring of congratulatory media stories featuring joyful ethnic minorities, good comrades and citizens and glorious historical deeds. Meanwhile Tiananmen Square, which is the heart of the great people's revolution, was firmly sealed and off limits.

In March, I had dinner in a noisy Korean barbecue restaurant in Beijing with a favourite Chinese artist. Only 32 years old, he already enjoys a successful international career, is profoundly patriotic and the holder of an important teaching post. During the evening, my friend passionately expounded an opinion in full earshot of fellow diners and waiting staff that would have made me extremely uncomfortable even five years ago. Namely, that the Chinese Communist Party in 2011 is more fundamentally corrupt than even Chiang Kai-shek's Kuomintang (KMT or Nationalist Party) of the 40s. The official history, tirelessly propagated in films and TV dramas, is that that the nationalist administration had degenerated into a kind of murderous gangsterism before the 1949 revolution. Yet my artist friend argued that pre-revolutionary society in many ways remained, for all its faults, a pluralistic one: an imperfect democracy. There was at least formal acknowledgment of the independence of the judiciary and channels to seek redress from injustice. The Communist Party of the 21st century, on the other hand, retains its monopoly on power through intimidation and force. It is deeply complicit in land grabs, forced evictions, endemic bribery and corruption. It even facilitates the enrichment of favoured businesses through official contracts and privileged access to resources and markets.

Ai Weiwei: 'Moon Chest' detail, 2008, Huanghvali wood, 81 pieces, 320 x 160 x 180cm
Courtesy: Lisson Gallery/the artist

The legal system today, my friend told me, is explicitly in place in order to serve the interests of the Party above anything else. Citizens who attempt to petition the government to redress flagrant social wrongs can expect to be met at best with official obstruction. In many documented cases they will encounter thuggish intimidation and violence. This viewpoint is not unusual. In a way that is entirely characteristic of China, I then went on to hear the same, previously unimaginable, opinion expressed by three other, unrelated people within the course of as many weeks. If during the course of conversation with people in China, one digs just a little, it's possible to encounter a profound and worrying cynicism in the integrity of the Chinese state.

It seems that suddenly these views are being expressed loudly and in public. Ai Weiwei, on the other hand, has been consistently and persistently making his views known. His father, Ai Qing, was one of China's most eminent poets, but was a political prisoner for 16 years in the western desert region of Xinjiang. This is where Ai Weiwei spent his entire childhood and early adolescence. When Ai Weiwei returned to China in 1993 after ten years in the United States, his rehabilitated father advised him on his responsibility as a Chinese citizen to speak out, reportedly saying, 'You are at home here, there's no need to be polite.'

An intriguingly enigmatic artist, Ai Weiwei's public personality is also complex and elusive. The true Ai Weiwei may well be a nuanced combination of the many faults of which his detractors accuse him. However, it has also now become clear, even to his harshest critics, that this artist has courageously maintained a highly principled position for which he is now paying a heavy price. It is my observation that many others are beginning to come round to his point of view. ❐

40(3): 20/33
DOI 10.1177/0306422011419122
www.indexoncensorship.org

Simon Kirby is the director of Chambers Fine Art in Beijing

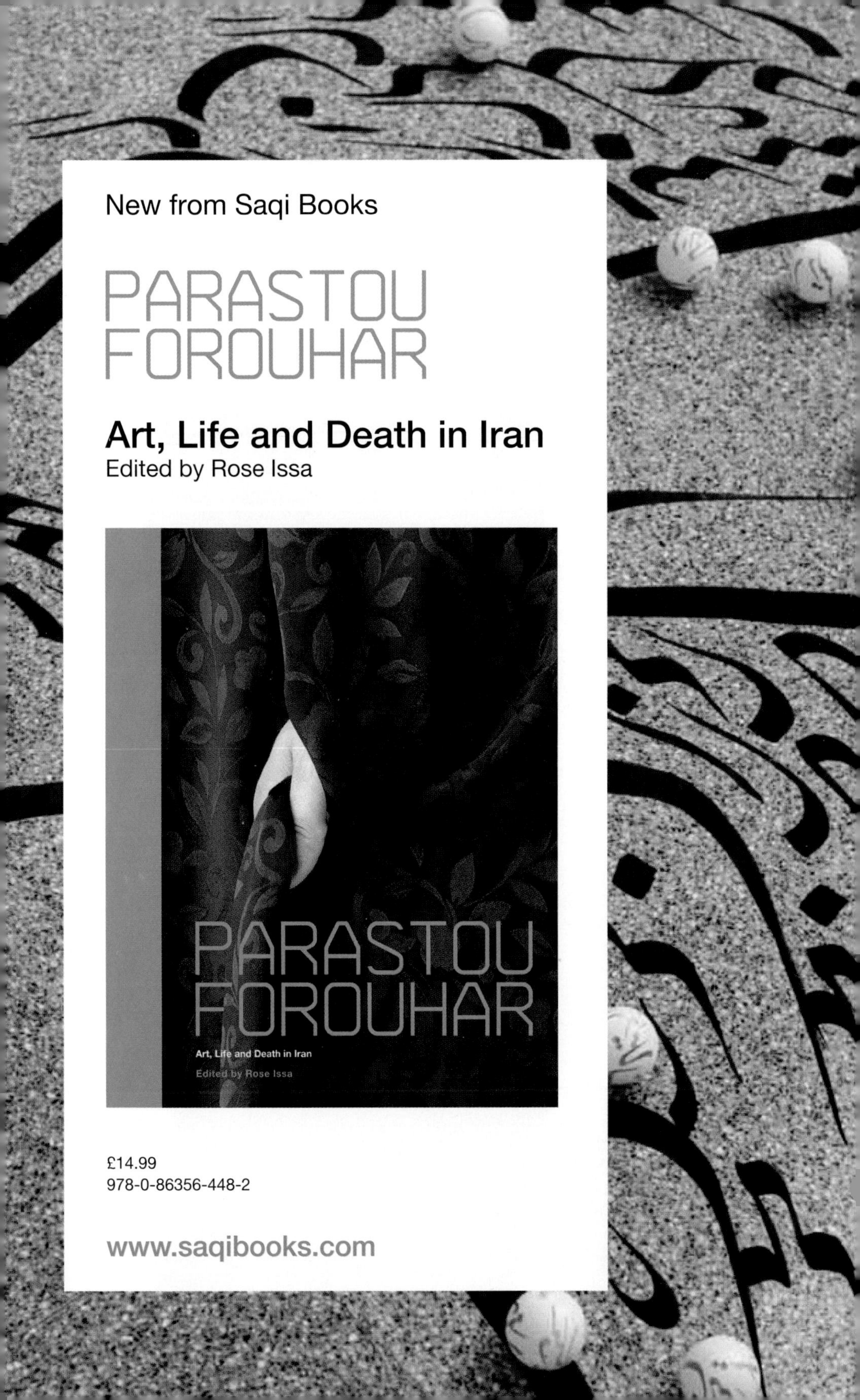
New from Saqi Books
PARASTOU FOROUHAR
Art, Life and Death in Iran
Edited by Rose Issa
PARASTOU FOROUHAR
Art, Life and Death in Iran
Edited by Rose Issa
£14.99
978-0-86356-448-2
www.saqibooks.com

Papa Benedetto XVI

PICTURE THIS

Malu Halasa on
'Lollipope' by Parastou Forouhar

Readers of *Parastou Forouhar: Art, Life and Death in Iran*, edited by Rose Issa, will come to the end of a lavishly illustrated 128-page monograph on one of the country's best known contemporary conceptual artists and find the last page somehow stuck to the book's inside back cover. At first it seems as if a mishap occurred at the printers. But on further investigation, it becomes quickly apparent that this page had been glued on purpose and the end image, captioned '"Lollipope", a digital print on Alu Dibond 65cm × 45cm (2008)', had been vandalised. Black ink covers the face of a woman in a black, flower-patterned *chador*. What has been obscured is that she is licking a lollipop showing the benign, smiling image of Pope Benedictus XVI, or Benedetto XVI, as he is known affectionately to the Catholic faithful, kitsch confection sold to tourists at the Vatican.

Black marks over the faces and bodies of women photographed in western magazines imported into the Middle East, particularly the Gulf states, are not unusual. But art books published in Lebanon usually leave the country unscarred by the authorities. Forouhar's photograph, less about flesh and more about an irreverent attitude toward religion, upset Lebanese censors. 'They didn't like the image,' explained Salwa Gaspard, director of Saqi Books, the monograph's publishers. 'They said it was offensive for the book and the veiled woman.' She later clarified in an email: '[From] the airport they sent the boxes of books back to us, then two men came the next day to the office, and asked for us to cover the picture with black ink, and glue the two pages.'

Every book exported from Lebanon is examined in the office of Surete Generale (General Security) at Beirut-Rafic Hariri International airport before a consignment leaves the country. The titles that normally cause problems for Saqi, pioneer publishers in the region, 'are mainly those on politics and religion, not so much art', observed Gaspard in the interview,

'Lollipope', a digital print on Alu Dibond 65cm × 45cm, 2008
Credit: Parastou Farouhar

'because artists usually censor themselves. They know they cannot have a lot of nudes. Usually we know what will happen but this book caught us by surprise.'

Once a judgment is made, there is no way to appeal the decision, unless a publisher is jailed. All over the Middle East, censors vet new books by Arab authors and most of them are not allowed into their respective countries. Gaspard cited the case of the poet and politician Ghazi Algosaibi, the Labour minister of Saudi Arabia, whose books were banned from that country until two weeks before his death in 2010. Now it seems that some art books won't be allowed into the West for its own protection. Despite all her experience of censorship and Arab regimes, the furore surrounding 'Lollipope' still baffled Gaspard. 'You wouldn't imagine that in the Arab world this image would be seen as offensive. The artist didn't make the lollipop. It's something anyone can buy.'

Because of the censorship, the monograph didn't arrive in time for Forouhar's exhibition at Leighton House in London in 2010. Born in 1962, she studied art in Tehran and Germany. In the current art boom of Iranian art, she has emerged as an engaged, thought-provoking artist who addresses themes of state brutality and the religious repression of women in remarkable work, which ranges from installation, performance and calligraphy to textile and furniture design and photography. In 1998, her parents, Dariush and Parvaneh Forouhar were savagely murdered at home during a spate of unsolved killings of intellectuals in Tehran known as the Chain Murders. Dariush Forouhar, who had been imprisoned under the Shah, served for six months in the new government following the 1979 Islamic revolution before he resigned. His and his wife's murders, along with the others, were eventually blamed by the regime on rogue agents in the Ministry of Intelligence.

In the monograph, Forouhar is quoted as saying, 'My efforts to investigate this crime had a great impact on my personal and artistic sensibilities. Political correctness and democratic coexistence lost their meaning in my daily life. As a result, I have tried to distil this conflict of displacement and transfer of meaning, turning it into a source of creativity.' When she was told of the Lebanese government's censorship of 'Lollipope', she laughed, according to the book's editor Rose Issa, who added that the artist has an incredible sense of humour.

Issa continued, 'Parastou, who lives in Germany, visits Iran regularly. When she returns home for the anniversary of her parents' death, the authorities close the street where they live to visitors and only people under guard are allowed on that street. She refuses to have a German passport. By losing her Iranian passport and becoming a German resident, she can lose her parents' house.'

For Issa, the curator of Forouhar's Leighton House exhibition who has been instrumental in introducing Iranian and Arab art to the West, there are many more images in the monograph that are potentially more disturbing. That the Lebanese censors picked 'Lollipope' remains a mystery, one she openly dismissed: 'It takes a sophisticated mind to see, for example, "Parvaneh".' This series by Forouhar, named after her mother, means 'butterfly'in Farsi. It shows seemly whimsical and decorative butterflies when viewed from afar that become, on closer inspection, stylised representations of people under torture. Issa then posed the billion-dollar question: 'A veiled woman licking a lollipop, on what level did it hurt them?' ❐

40(3): 34/37
DOI: 10.1177/0306422011418411
www.indexoncensorship.org

Malu Halasa is an author, editor and journalist. Her books include *Transit Tehran* (Garnet) and *The Secret Life of Syrian Lingerie* (Chronicle)

CULTURE WARS

A censorship scandal at one of the leading public institutions in the US is a setback for artistic and academic freedom, says **Philip Kennicott**

When David Wojnarowicz made *Fire In My Belly*, an opened-ended video project that occupied him from 1986–7, a positive diagnosis for HIV was almost assuredly a death sentence. Wojnarowicz, an artist-provocateur who openly identified with 'sexual outlaws' and had a long-standing and artistically productive love-hate relationship with the Catholic Church, lost his lover to Aids in 1987, the same year he learned that he too had the virus. Made with footage filmed in Mexico, and rich with images of violence and earthy Christianity, the video included scenes of martyrs, wrestling, cockfighting, blood dripping into bowls and a brief passage, about 14 seconds long, that showed ants crawling on a crucifix.

An excerpt of Wojnarowicz's video was included at a small viewing kiosk as part of an exhibition devoted to images of gay and lesbian people mounted at the Smithsonian Institution's National Portrait Gallery in Washington, DC in October 2010. *Hide/Seek: Difference and Desire in the American Portraiture* was the first serious exploration of art made by or about gay and lesbian people launched in an American museum since 1982, when New York's New Museum hosted *Extended Sensibilities*, a snapshot of camp, artifice and naughtiness that defined the 'gay' aesthetic before Aids. Critics hailed the Smithsonian show for its comprehensive survey of American art, its dispassionate tone and for the care with which it explored the cultural evolution of the idea of homosexual or gay identity. The curators, Jonathan D Katz and David C Ward, introduced audiences to a brilliant but hidden history of desire and art, carefully explaining complicated ideas about the social construct of sexuality that were only just beginning to migrate from the academy to a broader general understanding.

But the Wojnarowicz video offered an opening for culturally conservative critics to attack the exhibition, and in December 2010 they succeeded in re-igniting the culture wars that had largely died out in America for a decade or more. A conservative website brought the ants-and-crucifix scene to the attention of William Donohue, leader of the right-wing Catholic League, which denounced the video as anti-Catholic and enlisted the support of conservative leaders of the newly Republican-dominated House of Representatives. Although the exhibition had been financed with private donations, there were threats of eliminating public funding to the entire Smithsonian, which operates a complex of museums, a zoo and research institutions around the country and in Panama. Popular media demagogues, including Glenn Beck, seized on the issue, and within hours of the first reports that the Smithsonian had mounted an 'anti-Christian' exhibition, the secretary of the Smithsonian, G Wayne Clough, removed the video.

Clough's decision to censor one of his institution's most highly-regarded shows in years was made despite the vehement objections of his own curators and professional staff. He defended it as a pragmatic, surgical response, designed to defuse the controversy before it threatened the larger exhibition and the institution itself. While it appeased Donohue, the decision to censor was widely denounced throughout the museum world, with clarity and vehemence by organisations such as the Association of Art Museum Directors, and with tepid, bureaucratic language by more quietist organisations such as the American Association of Museums. Within the gay community there was especial anger, uniting activists of an older generation who knew the scourge of Aids first-hand and younger gays and lesbians (and their supporters) who were astonished to see the bigotry of the 80s and 90s reanimated within the Smithsonian. The museum was caught off guard, unable to defend what might have been viewed as a pragmatic trade-off a decade ago – a little anti-gay censorship in exchange for the good will of mounting a largely 'pro-gay' exhibition – to a new generation that seemed to believe that the acceptable amount of homophobia in a public museum was now zero.

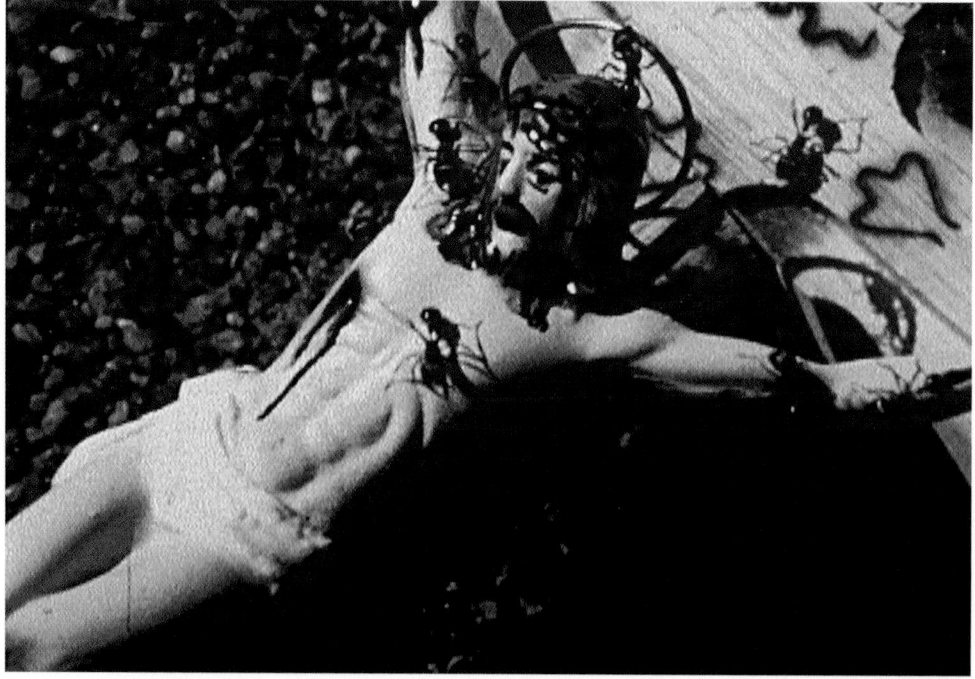

But the decision to censor went far beyond the cultural politics of Catholicism and homosexuality. It was disastrous for the Smithsonian, on a tactical and strategic level. Worse, it threatened to advance an argument against public funding for education and the arts into the realm of all educational and cultural organisations that receive any funding, directly or indirectly, from public sources. Clough had not only reignited the culture wars, he had brought their fury right to the gates of academia, tacitly acceding to an argument that could now be used successfully against almost every educational and cultural institution in the United States.

Clough brought the culture wars to the gates of academia

Two broad social trends made the Smithsonian's censorship scandal particularly surprising. Attitudes to homosexuality had grown increasingly tolerant over the last quarter century, with a marked acceleration of tolerance in the past two years. The culture wars, which had been particularly fuelled by the conservative critique of gay rights, were also largely over. Museums, in particular, had enjoyed more than a decade without any serious crisis over content or free expression. Since 1969, when New York's Metropolitan Museum of Art angered African-Americans with *Harlem on My Mind*, an exhibition about black life in Harlem that excluded input from African-American artists, museums had been a favourite site for cultural conflict, for both the right and the left. The right wing largely dominated debates about content in the 80s and 90s, but since 1999, when the Brooklyn Museum of Art also ran afoul of Donohue and the Catholic League with *Sensation*, an exhibition of art owned by Charles Saatchi, there had been remarkably little museum controversy.

In 2009, Stephen Dubin, author of *Displays of Power*, an historical survey of museum debates, offered one explanation for the seeming cessation of hostilities. 'From 1989 to 2001, we had no external enemy,' said Dubin, of the period during which such crises were at their most volatile. With the attacks of 11 September 2001, cultural hostility turned outward, to 'terrorists', and in many pockets of American culture, to Islam. Many of the cultural conflicts

David Wojnarowicz, A Fire In My Belly (Film in Progress) *and* A Fire In My Belly Excerpt, *1986–87*
Super 8mm film transferred to video (black and white and colour, silent), 13:06 mins. and 7:00 mins.
Courtesy of the Estate of David Wojnarowicz and PPOW Gallery, New York and The Fales Library and Special Collections/New York University

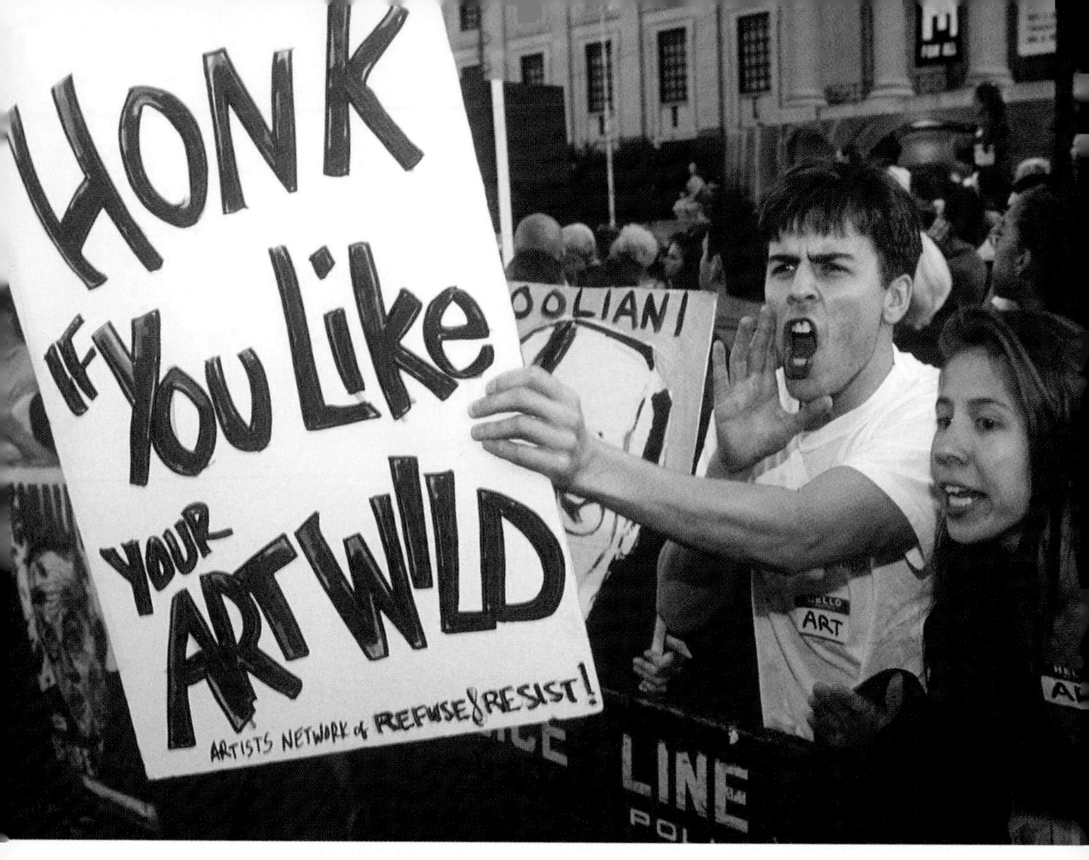

Demonstration outside the Brooklyn Museum, New York, during the Sensation *exhibition, 1999*
Credit: Sipa Press/Rex Features

that were fought in museums also shifted to other areas of public discourse, as the country fought a real war over gay marriage rather than symbolic wars of images of gay and lesbian people in museums. The internet and cable television also offered new outlets for cultural rancour, perhaps acting as a pressure valve on museums.

But museum leaders had also learned substantial lessons about public discourse from the culture wars and, in many ways, they became more adept at dealing with debates over content and requests to censor. In the spring of 2002, the Jewish Museum in New York came under fire for an exhibition called *Mirroring Evil*, which included the work of 13 young artists who were grappling with the persistent power of Nazi iconography in contemporary art. Descriptions of the show offended some survivors of the Holocaust, and the media fanned the flames with talk of 'the next art-world *Sensation*', an explicit reference to the Brooklyn controversy of 1999. But the Jewish Museum successfully defused hostility by hosting panel discussions and other public events, acknowledging that controversy was an essential part of the museum's mission, and thus reinforcing the often frail commitment of museums to free speech. 'It quieted down within a few weeks after the show opened, once people saw the work and engaged in the interpretive process,' said Joan Rosenbaum, the museum's director.

The speed with which Clough censored the *Hide/Seek* exhibition suggested ignorance of this decade-long history of successful adaptation within the museum world. Although Clough's fear of the new Republican majority in the Congress was reasonable, there was little evidence that the public had any appetite for another round of museum battles. The primary public concern at the time was the economy and the ongoing wars in Iraq and Afghanistan. Tactically, Clough retreated from a conflict he likely could have won. Strategically, he blundered because he put the larger museum world in jeopardy of similar attacks. He also failed to use the inherent power of the museum and its curators in vigorous defence of the museum's agenda, and its essential value: free speech.

All it took was a megaphone and access to Congress

The ambiguous content of the Wojnarowicz video – its idiosyncratic use of religious imagery – and a powerful commentary on these images left by Wojnarowicz before he died in 1992 gave Smithsonian officials substantial material with which to defend the video against charges of sacrilege or anti-Catholic bias. Wojnarowicz was assuredly anti-Catholic, but was anti-Catholic within a long-standing tradition of Catholics using Catholic iconography to call for reform of the Church. The Smithsonian was in an excellent position to offer a history lesson about the Aids crisis, foster dialogue about religion, engage a wider public and re-enforce a complicated cultural habit: acceptance of the museum as a privileged public space for controversy. Clough's deletion of the video from the exhibition compromised long-standing efforts by museum directors around the country to position their institutions as laboratories for social research, sometimes controversial.

The symbolic power of Clough's rapid capitulation was enormous. The Smithsonian is the largest complex of museums and research institutions

"Jews don't like images," I said,
"because images are charged
was cold,
really talk,
9 781570 270468
Jim Fleming
Believing in the transcendental power
of the image and it's Beauty is like wanting to be an
Abstract Expressionist or a Cowboy."

in the world. It is no stranger to censorship, but this time the stakes were higher than in past controversies. Although the Smithsonian had effectively censored a 2003 exhibition of photographs of a threatened wildlife refuge in the Arctic, the organisation was able to justify its actions based on putative uncertainty about the science of global warming. With the removal of the Wojnarowicz video, however, Clough was simply acceding to the demands of a small but vocal group that had made its reputation (and enjoyed considerable economic success) with a hit-and-run strategy of complaint against major cultural organisations. All it took, apparently, to demand changes to Smithsonian content, was a megaphone and access to members of Congress. It was a devastating precedent.

Few, if any debates about censorship in the United States fall neatly into clean divisions between advocates for and against free speech. As a spokesman for former New York Senator Alfonse D'Amato said in 1988: 'He is absolutely opposed to censorship, but we are talking about taxpayers' dollars.' D'Amato, at the time, was leading the charge to censor an exhibition of photographs by Robert Mapplethorpe, on display at another Washington museum, the Corcoran Gallery of Art. Most debates about free speech within the museum world have hinged on D'Amato's distinction. As they did with the Mapplethorpe case, cultural conservatives positioned their concerns about *Hide/Seek* as an issue of public funding and government-sponsored speech, not a clear-cut case of censorship.

Since the Mapplethorpe controversy and subsequent attacks on the National Endowment for the Arts, museums have fought a mostly losing battle to convince the public that they should receive public funding, yet still be given full freedom to exhibit controversial art and discuss unpopular ideas. If the debate hinges on a simple principle – should public funds be used to support art and ideas that offend the public? – museums always lose.

But if the argument is framed more broadly, public support for controversial material in museums can co-exist with government funding. This argument relies not on a single, easy to grasp principle with powerful emotional appeal – I shouldn't have to pay for art that offends me – but a series of propositions about public life and the role museums play in it: that museums are essential educational, cultural and social institutions; that the work they do best can't be done without insulation from the market economy; that not everything they do will please every audience; that public funding is in support not of a particular message, but rather of an open arena for diverse messages.

Mirroring Evil *exhibition at the Jewish Museum, New York, 22 March 2002*
Credit: Sipa Press/Rex Features

In the decade before December 2010, many museums had worked diligently to demonstrate the force of these principles through action and engagement. Remarkably, in 2009, when the American economy was in deep recession, museum attendance rose across all categories and sizes surveyed by the American Association of Museums. The fruits of museum reform – in particular, a commitment to remove perceived cultural and social barriers to attendance – were beginning to be felt. Although the economics of museum survival were still complicated and tenuous, they were in the best position in years to defend their values and prerogatives in case of new controversy over content.

Clough's decision undercut a slowly built social praxis of engagement with museums as a safe place within democracy for the discussion of complicated and contentious ideas. An innate American suspicion of authority has both furthered and often hindered museums' efforts to occupy this space. Small nuances in how a museum's role is framed can make all the difference in the public's support of its mission. 'Exploration' and 'understanding', which suggest self-directed learning, engage fundamentally American values of freedom and self-improvement. 'Teaching' and 'education' often provoke resistance for their presumed submission to authority figures. Museums that allow narratives of social inequity to unfold in familiar or sympathetic voices often engage successfully with audiences; didactic presentation of the same material usually fails.

The *Hide/Seek* exhibition was organised with a subtle understanding of how controversial subject matter can be freely presented in a museum that is also a publicly supported institution. Clough's censorship of it was apparently done without a broader sense of the recent social history of the museum, and the considerable success museums were having with the complicated dance they must perform in a democracy. The broader danger of Clough's decision to set the clocks back in a very public and symbolic way, to re-engage the dynamics of the culture wars, and to give institutional support to the anti-museum principle of no government support for controversial speech (as opposed to the slowly inculcated cultural habit of support for the historic humanist ideals of the museum), will likely be to the institution from which Clough came: academia. The very same set of assumptions upon which freedom of speech within publicly supported museums is based (insulation from the market, acceptance of unpopular or controversial avenues of research) is also essential to almost every academic institution in the United States. The basic argument used against museums so effectively – no public support for controversial work – can just

'Women against pornography' badge, New York, October 1979
Credit: Hulton Archive/Getty Images

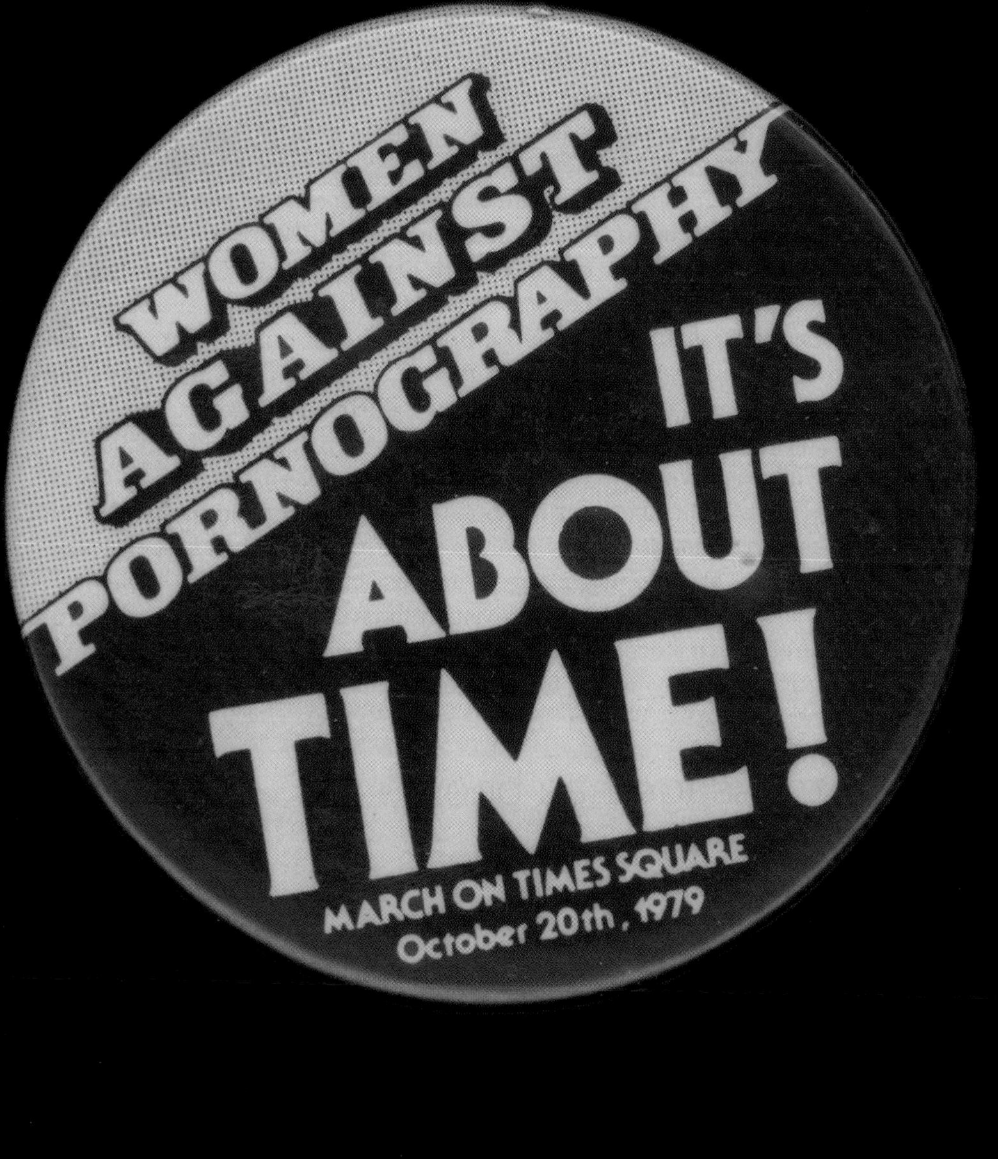

WOMEN AGAINST PORNOGRAPHY

IT'S ABOUT TIME!

MARCH ON TIMES SQUARE

October 20th, 1979

as easily be used against universities, most of which receive at least some kind of government support. The same unstable coalition of political forces that came together to attack museums – cultural conservatives, small-government fiscal hawks, anti-authoritarian populists, anti-elitist demagogues – could very easily be assembled in an effective and concerted attack on public funding for universities.

Because of the substantial support the Smithsonian receives from the US government – more than $750m in 2010 – the censorship of *Hide/Seek* can't be framed as a simple debate about free expression, even if the exhibition was privately funded. But analysed as a social performance, a publicly enacted drama, the events look very much like a classic case of American censorship. From the Palmer Raids of 1919–20 (prompted by fears of anarchism) to the Patriot Act of 2001, major inroads against free speech have generally been spurred by harnessing public fear. Clough's rapid decision to remove material from the exhibition was premised on his fear for the institution's financial wellbeing at a time of political upheaval and economic uncertainty. From the Comstock Laws of 1873 to the quixotic feminist campaign against pornography a century later, censorship has thrived during periods of sexual hysteria, and often at the expense of sexual minorities. Although Clough's censorship was framed as a response to religious concerns, he may have expected it to be broadly palatable to the public because of the long-standing power of homophobia within American culture. And as in so many dramas of censorship and campaigns against free speech, it was presented as an exceptional case. 'The possibility of this ever happening again is extremely remote,' said Clough in an interview after the controversy. Yet even if it doesn't happen again, a message has already been sent: unpopular ideas may not be tolerated at the Smithsonian.

A message has been sent: unpopular ideas may not be tolerated

The Smithsonian's institutional response seems to bear out that dark possibility. On 31 January, the institution released a brief report on the crisis, neither absolving nor condemning Clough for his decision to censor. Most of the report fell back on the usual recommendations that large bureaucratic organisations rely on to give the appearance of learning from crisis: better and clearer lines of communication, improved public engagement. The three-member panel that examined Clough's decision appeared to issue an important endorsement of free speech within the museum system. They wrote that 'in the absence of actual error, changes to exhibitions should not be made once an exhibition opens', but they also added a caveat: '... without meaningful consultation with the curator, director, secretary, and the leadership of the Board of Regents'.

More troubling, the panel's efforts to promote better communication also seemed to call for the creation of *ad hoc* bodies which might have the power to veto content or intimidate curators: 'in anticipation of possibly controversial exhibitions, the Smithsonian should provide an opportunity for public input or reaction at pre-decisional exhibit planning phases'. They also called for a broad survey of upcoming exhibitions and programmes, looking forward three years, 'to assess the curriculum against ... the nation's agenda, and potential controversies'.

The report only confused the situation, making it unclear whether the Smithsonian and its leadership is committed primarily to institutional survival, or if it holds higher values, including a vigorous commitment to free speech. In the aftermath of the controversy, Clough never apologised for the censorship, nor engaged in a substantial exchange about when, and under what conditions, he would censor in the future. That lack of clarity may well be strategic, a chilling and intentional uncertainty introduced into the institution to keep all of its curators aware of invisible lines that must never be crossed. Or it may simply be the reflexive habit of cultural leaders who simply want the crisis to go away. So far the two things that might undo some of the damage have yet to happen: a full, honest, open account of the decision, and a statement of unambiguous commitment to academic and curatorial freedom in the future. As it stands now, the most important public educational and museum institution in the United States has demonstrated an uncertain commitment to the basic values of enlightened and free discourse. ❐

40(3): 38/49
DOI:10.1177/0306422011419123
www.indexoncensorship.org

Philip Kennicott is chief art critic of the *Washington Post*

Martha Wilson
September 9 – October 8, 2011
P·P·O·W
I have become my own worst fea
535 West 22nd St, 3rd Floor
New York, NY 10011
T 212 647 1044
F 212 941 8643
www.ppowgallery.com

ART LESSONS

There's a difference between being an advocate and a player in the free speech wars. **John Frohnmayer** reports on how to survive a political ambush

If you are a citizen of the United States, you have the privilege of being offended. If you never are, the First Amendment is not working because you are not hearing the voices of dissent, of outrage and of consummate stupidity. To elevate offence – to offer protection from it – above free speech inverts the First Amendment, which protects the speaker from government interference. Always.

The tough issues arise when the subject matter is raw and the speaker is a minority, or is obnoxious, unlikeable, angry and rude. And when such a speaker is supported by tax dollars, as is the case with the National Endowment for the Arts (NEA), it is easy for an elected official to play to the grandstands, as did Senator Jesse Helms in proposing restrictive (and unconstitutional) legislation in 1989: 'If senators want the federal government funding pornography, sadomasochism, or art for paedophiles, they should vote against my bill.'

Never mind that the perceived offences caused by the work of Robert Mapplethorpe and Andres Serrano, who also saw funding for their work cut by the NEA, represented only a couple of grants out of 100,000. Never

Installation views from Witnesses: Against Our Vanishing, *Artists Space, New York, 16 November 1989-6 January 1990. Photo: Frances Miller Smith*

mind that the cross in Serrano's 'Piss Christ' is a symbol of rejection, pain and death, not some sugar-coated trinket to hang around the neck; and never mind that the government cannot be in the business of deciding what is and is not blasphemy precisely because the First Amendment says Congress shall make no law about religion, speech, press, petition or assembly.

The First Amendment recognises that freedom of spirit is the fundamental ingredient of human dignity, and as such, it applies to everyone, not just those with whom we agree. (Whether it should apply to those that do not breathe, like the corporations the Supreme Court has recently enfranchised, is another matter entirely.)

That is all theory, but this is a personal account of one who was ambushed in a First Amendment battle. I wish I could say that I fought nobly and well, but, with several decades' hindsight, I should have done better, as should the current secretary of the Smithsonian, who recently found himself

in a similar battle, which goes to show that what we know about history is that we don't learn anything from it.

Within two weeks of my arrival in Washington as the newly minted chairman of the National Endowment for the Arts, I was approached by a grant recipient, Artists Space in New York City, who worried that their show on Aids included a catalogue essay that was inflammatory. The author was none other than David Wojnarowicz, the same of the recent controversy of the Smithsonian show *Hide/Seek*, which was attacked for being 'an outrageous use of taxpayer money' by one politician and re-ignited the debate about public arts funding.

I should have said: 'That grant has already been given; it is not my problem.' Instead I suspended the grant without seeing the show, I made stupid statements about how the art was political, I shot myself in the foot repeatedly and finally, having destroyed my credibility with most everyone, restored the grant. My First Amendment principles were in the lost and found.

What follows is not – I repeat, not – an excuse. It is, however, a reality. Everything in Washington is political, and that includes the First Amendment. Shortly before the Artists Space matter, Congress had whacked $45,000 off the Endowment's budget, an amount exactly equalling the grants to the shows that included Mapplethorpe and Serrano. Representative Charles Stenholm of Texas, arguing for the cut, said: 'Political pressure – you better believe it. ... I am here to participate in putting political pressure and believe that to be anything but censorship.' President George Bush's chief of staff made a point of telling me how much of a problem the artists were for the administration, and the national uproar was consuming. Congress got more mail about the National Endowment in 1990 than it did about the Savings and Loan crisis of the late 80s and early 90s. Just to put that in monetary perspective, the S & L debacle cost every taxpayer about $3,000 and the Endowment, for everything we did in a year, cost 68 cents. Pressure? I believed it.

I broke out in a rash, couldn't sleep, didn't know who to listen to, and everywhere I went I was hounded by reporters. And I had considered myself a First Amendment lawyer. There is a vast difference, I found, between being an advocate and being a player in the First Amendment game.

So here are a few thoughts on how I could have done better.

First, come out swinging. If a grant has been given, it went through a rigorous process and was found worthy (and by the way, was found to have artistic content and therefore could not, by definition, be obscene). You might not want the picture over your fireplace, but somebody else might not groove on Mozart.

Defend the First Amendment, not the specific artwork. Rally your allies outside the realm of the arts – the librarians and labour unions and pastors and teachers. Be quotable because the battle is, on some level, for public opinion and the principle of not censoring is much bigger than any piece of art.

Art is meant to get a reaction. We shouldn't be surprised when it does. But when the attack is pitched on moral grounds, then the rejoinder has to be a careful distinction between the roles of law and morality in our society. The law tells you what you can and can't do and if you transgress, you go to jail. Morality commands what you should or shouldn't do, but your reward or punishment will be in some other sphere. Artists using public dollars are protected by the First Amendment. Critics arguing morality can preen in indignation, but they have no legal standing to support their outrage.

Do your damage control drills before the crisis hits. Who gathers information? Who talks to the trustees, the university president, the sheriff, the District Attorney? Who talks to the press, and who feeds information to friendly sources; who blogs and twitters? I mean actually practise, not just think about it. Role play. Rehearse.

Finally, prepare to get fired. Once it became clear to me that I probably would be fired (about nine months into the job), I was liberated to do the job right. And when I was ultimately fired, it was for defending the First Amendment, not cowering from it. Cervantes anticipated the substance of the First Amendment in Don Quixote: 'The enchanters may rob me of good fortune, but never of my spirit or my will.' ❐

DOI 10.1177/0306422011418148
40(3): 51/55
www.indexoncensorship.org

John Frohnmayer was the chair of the National Endowment for the Arts during the first Bush administration. A lawyer and writer, he is the author of *Leaving Town Alive: Confessions of an Arts Warrior* (Houghton Mifflin) and *Out of Tune: Listening to the First Amendment* (Fulcrum)

RELICS OF FREEDOM

Artists today are on a collision course with religious sensibilities. **Matthew Bown** considers what happens when the cult of the body goes global

In 2006, in my gallery in Savile Row, I put on a show by the artist Arnis Balčus featuring works from *Killing Rampage*. It's a narrative made up of black-and-white photos that imitate film stills; they evoke a Russ Meyer-type movie in which three sexily clad or unclad young women go around shooting people. In 2009 I received the following email:

> My name is Sabine and I was model for Arnis Balčus photo-story *Killing Rampage* (the blonde girl).
>
> Photos of his work *Episodes* were exhibited in your gallery on year 2006 and they can also be seen on your web-sight.
>
> The thing is that I'm becoming a Muslim and as you maybe know, it's absolutely unacceptable for Muslim woman to be seen publicly this much uncovered.
>
> My request to You is to be responsive and remove those pictures of *Killing Rampage* where I can be seen or at least cancel the option where they can be enlarged.

Titian's 'Venus of Urbino', Galleria delgi Uffizi, Florence, Italy
Credit: Superstock/Alamy

Please. It is really important for me.

Hoping for Your understanding and praying

I spoke to Balčus and we decided to help Sabine out. I didn't want to scramble her new life, whatever I might have thought of the ideas that she was committing to. But it made me wonder about the line that Sabine was crossing, which involved in effect her re-writing of her own life story. Once upon a time, for a minimal fee (Balčus tended to pay his performers £20), she had agreed to be photographed in raunchy scenarios for an artwork that was published widely, as a book and in a gallery and on the internet. She did it, presumably, for 'art', in the narrow sense of helping out Balčus and in the broader one of building her own career as an actress. And then along came a religion – to be precise, Islam – and it had something to say that conflicted with what art had to say: about whether she could 'be seen publicly this much uncovered'.

The cult of the body

One of the key disputes in the Christian Church during its first thousand years or so was over the *filioque* clause added in 589 to the Nicene Creed, *filioque* meaning 'and the son' and signifying that the third part of the Holy Trinity, the Holy Ghost, issued from the Father *and* the Son, as opposed to both Son and Ghost issuing from the Father. The Church wrangled over these alternatives for centuries, and the dispute led eventually to the Great Schism between the Latin and Greek churches of 1054. The Latin Church confirmed the *filioque*; the Greek Orthodox Church rejected it. Recognition of the *filioque* meant making the Father and Son equivalent, and as a result making the physical forms of God and Man equivalent, thus providing theological support for the Renaissance revival of the ancient cult of the body, which could be derived technically from Greek and Roman art. As soon as the realistic depiction of Christ was allowed, it became implicitly a sexualised depiction, one that the art historian Leo Steinberg analysed in his classic essay *The Sexuality of Christ in Renaissance Art and in Modern Oblivion* (1983).

The balance of spiritual power shifted to art

Mary the Mother of God was no less of a pin-up: the fundamentalist preacher Savonarola, who was burned at the stake in Florence in 1498, complained about modern painters who 'made the Virgin Mary look like a harlot'. Pagan imagery provided Renaissance artists with endless pretexts for orgiastic subjects. Everyday-life nudes such as Titian's 'Venus of Urbino' situated erotic nudity squarely in the modern world. The Council of Trent (1545–63), the main conference of the Counter Reformation, clamped down on this sort of stuff in a Catholic context, but by then the process of accommodation between Christianity and the naked figure and all it entailed was firmly established: it was a matter of negotiation. The Enlightenment sent religion into terminal decline as an intellectual force. Romanticism shifted the balance of spiritual power to art. The post-Romantic successor to Michelangelo's entirely nude 'Christ Carrying the Cross' in Santa Maria sopra Minerva, Rome (the penis was knocked off by an irate visitor at some point, and subsequently a girdle was added), was Rodin's protean 'Balzac' nursing an erection under his great coat. If a conservative 19th-century painter wanted to depict a naked prostitute, he painted Mary Magdalene; if a radical painter wanted to do the same, he depicted a prostitute: the point is, everyone could do it.

There's nothing remotely like this centuries-long acculturation to representation, and the representation of sexuality, in Islamic culture. In Greek myths, eagerly revived in the Renaissance, artists made images so real they were thought to be alive. Mohammed, on the other hand, came down and said: 'Whoever makes a picture will be punished by Allah till he puts life in it, and he will never be able to put life in it.' The question of representation in Islam is complicated, but the depiction of living creatures by hand is discouraged in the Hadith and by Islamic authorities (images of the prophet, although they have existed for centuries, often with his face absent or obscured, are today unacceptable in some countries in the Middle East). Thus the central practice of western art down the ages, the depiction by hand of the human figure, has no real place in Islam. Strictly speaking, Sabine's objection to Balčus's work was not based on this teaching (in Islam various forms of reproductive imagery – photography, film, television, video – are in fact accepted, with conditions) but it certainly reflected the absence of the cult of the naked, sexualised body that is at the centre of the western tradition and which, before Sabine crossed over into Islam (I guess by marriage), had allowed her to be at ease with her image in Balčus's photos.

The politics of offence

Sabine's request was politely phrased and minor; the violent response to the Mohammed cartoons of 2005 was not. Islamic iconophobia, then, is accompanied by the potential for violence (this has probably been the perception in the West since the *fatwa* against Salman Rushdie, even though that concerned a literary work). This is a problem for the art world, the more so because the actual position of Islam regarding images is poorly understood (and that's assuming that there is a coherent position). The result is pre-emptive censorship in order to avoid upsetting Muslim sensibilities. In 2003, for example, Walsall Borough Council removed two images by the Russian art group AES from a show called *Veil* at the New Art Gallery. One, 'New Liberty, 2006', is an altered image of the Statue of Liberty, who now wears a *hijab* and carries a Quran under her arm. The other, 'London, 2006', features the Houses of Parliament with the domed roof of a mosque. The council justified its decision with a vague reference to 'political tensions'. At the 2005 Venice Biennale, the artist Gregor Schneider proposed the installation on St Mark's Square of a large black cube, to be made of cloth stretched over a scaffold, with the dimensions of the Kaaba, the building in Mecca, reputedly constructed by Abraham and his son Ishmael, that is the most sacred site in Islam (the Kaaba itself is draped with a curtain of black silk with gold embroidery). Schneider's project was cancelled by the Biennale organisers over terrorism fears and turned down again in Berlin in 2006. In January 2010, the Metropolitan Museum of Art in New York admitted it had removed all images depicting Mohammed from public display.

Another such incident occurred at this year's Venice Biennale. When Ilham Aliev, president of Azerbaijan, visited his country's pavilion prior to its official opening, he was confronted in the entrance hall by two sculptures in marble by Aidan Salakhova, an artist of Azerbaijani descent who works in Moscow, where she also owns and runs one of the city's leading contemporary art galleries. One, entitled 'Waiting Bride', showed a figure veiled from head to toe, only her hands being visible. The other was a representation of the Black Stone at Mecca that pilgrims, in imitation of the prophet Mohammed, stop to kiss, enclosed in a white frame whose form, to some viewers, resembled a schematic vagina (in fact, the silver setting of the Black Stone itself in Mecca perhaps fits this description even more closely). Aliev decided that both these works were unacceptable. He also decreed the removal of four works on paper by Salakhova with Islamo-erotic subjects, such as a woman wielding a minaret as a dildo. The sculptures were too big to move at short notice, so at the official opening of the pavilion they were concealed incongruously under sheets; later they were removed completely.

Arguably, these events are not censorship on religious grounds at all, they are the cautious decisions of wise cultural masters: councillors, biennale commissioners, a president. A kind of benign despotism. Aliev's reasoning, as reported in the press, reveals the dilemma faced by the president of a country balanced between the West and Islam. On the one hand, 'Praying Woman' was unacceptable because it suggested Azerbaijan was a benighted Muslim state, whereas it is officially secular. On the other hand, Salakhova's 'Black Stone' (which, given the requirement to kiss it, I suppose we have to interpret as an invitation to cunnilingus) he deemed offensive to Muslims. And in fairness to Aliev, he was certainly let down by his bureaucracy: they should have let him know what was coming. This was Venice, an international showcase: one cannot easily imagine the British pavilion featuring, say, pictures of a nun masturbating with a church steeple. But such events reveal how fragile are defences of artistic freedom; how ready those who might be expected to offer protection to art are to cede to merely the apprehension of pressure; how porous are the boundaries between contemporary art and geo-politics, particularly as contemporary art becomes a global phenomenon.

Piero Manzoni art auction at Sotheby's, London 1998
Credit: Nils Jorgensen/Rex Features

Taking over the sandpit

The western tradition deriving from the *filioque* doesn't have a monopoly in sexually explicit imagery. One can't imagine the Japanese withdrawing, as the Tate did in 2009, the catalogue to the *Pop Life* show because it included Richard Prince's moderately immodest photograph of the naked ten-year-old Brooke Shields (already shown widely, including at the New York Guggenheim). But the *filioque* had an influence that ranged wider than nudity in art. There's no equivalent, not only in Islam, but in other religious or cultural traditions, to the political and social consequences of the fusion of Man and God. Once you accept that Man is equivalent to God, then he is no longer the benighted subject of the Church; he can elevate his own qualities (Humanism), investigate creation (Enlightenment) and ultimately take over spiritual leadership (Romanticism). Art was integral to all this, it was the relics of these movements; and in the 20th century artists, encouraged by Marx and Freud, finally took over the spiritual sandpit from the martyrs,

'New Liberty, 2006'
Courtesy: Triumph Gallery, Moscow/AES+F

ايمكو
AGFA

confessors, seers, flagellants, ascetics and visionaries of organised Christianity. Art became the perfected instrument of personal liberation theology, which I'll call here PLT for short. This was liberation at every level: political, psychological, physiological. When in 1962–5 the Vatican II conference was further downplaying holy relics, Piero Manzoni was happily selling his own personal relics, shit in tins, literally for their weight in gold: the artworld was delighted, and still is – the Tate bought one in 2000. We scarcely notice any more how the world we live in has been shaped by art, as once it was shaped by Christian theology. Witness the broad demand for self-fulfilment (which gave us the 'Me Generation'), in the rise of such concepts as the 'self-starting' individual (required in every other job description), in celebrity culture shows that allow everyone their 15 minutes of fame as predicted by Andy Warhol, and in the whole devolution of life – including war, surgical procedures, crime, sexual congress and the act of dying – into spectacle, defined by Guy Debord as 'a social relation between people that is mediated by images'. The artist, then, provides a blueprint for modern man, just as did Jesus Christ in Thomas à Kempis's *De Imitatione Christi* in the 15th century.

In this negotiation with alien cultures are multiple conflicts

The heritage of PLT makes problematic the current expansion of contemporary art to countries that do not share the West's history of cultural development. This expansion is substantial. A panoply of commercial and non-commercial institutions has expanded to encompass lands that, maybe 20 years ago, showed no significant interest in contemporary art as it is understood in the West. Nowadays art fairs such as the Armory Show, Frieze and Art Basel compete with Art Dubai, Art HK (Hong Kong) and Art Shanghai. The London and New York auction houses hold specialist sales of Middle Eastern art and integrate Chinese artists into their contemporary sales; the Chinese auction market is now the third biggest after those of the US and the UK. A new outpost of the Guggenheim Museum has been mooted in Baku and one is due to open in Abu Dhabi in 2013. The Venice Biennale has expanded substantially in recent years to include pavilions by Central Asia, India, China, Saudi Arabia and other non-western countries.

'London, 2006'
Courtesy: Triumph Gallery, Moscow/AES+F

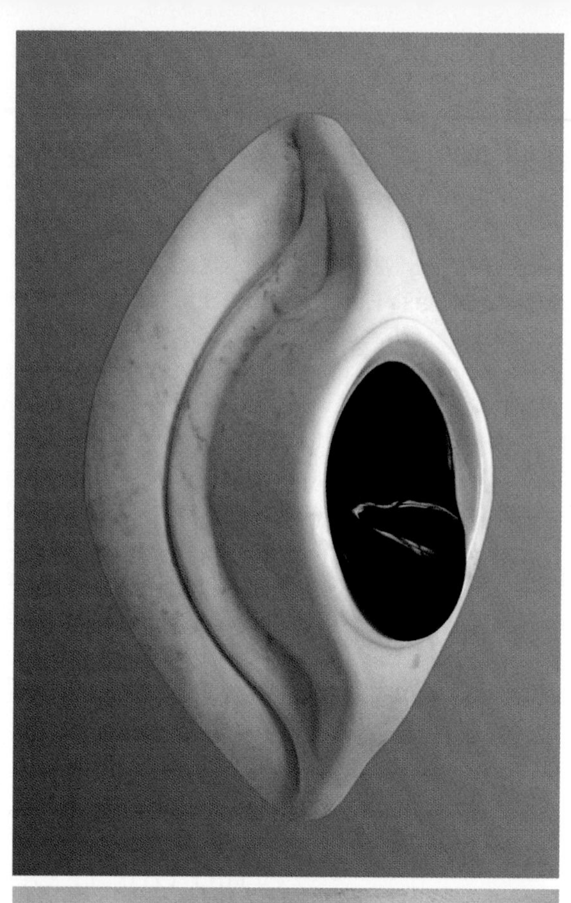

Aidan Salakhova: 'Waiting Bride' at the Azerbaijan National Pavilion, 54th International Art Exhibition of the Venice Biennial

I predict that as this expansion proceeds, one of two things will happen. Either countries resistant to PLT will adjust. Or else art itself will be adjusted. Probably a bit of both. Did the exhibition of work by Francis Bacon in Moscow in 1988, arranged by the British Council (and enabled, as it happens, by Aidan Salakhova's father Tair, then First Secretary of the USSR Artists' Union), contribute to the atmosphere that brought about the demise of the Soviet system? Quite possibly. On the other hand, the selection of work for the new Guggenheim Museum in Abu Dhabi is already being made with an eye to local sensibilities, i.e. to put it bluntly, the new collection is being pre-emptively censored.

If we accept that art is PLT, it must conflict with other belief systems; in this negotiation with alien cultures there will be multiple conflicts. A recent case in point is the arrest and recent release of China's most famous artist – at least the most famous in the West – Ai Weiwei. He was arrested because he had been too free in complaining about the lack of fundamental

Aidan Salakhova's 'The Black Stone', Destination series, 2010-2011. Marble, 125 × 75 × 40cm; 'The Book', Destination Series, 2010-2011. Marble 90 × 70 × 40 cm

freedoms in China. In other words, after considerable exposure to PLT he had *begun to think and behave like a westerner* (not all westerners of course), which is not possible in China. I was reminded of a comment that a Russian friend once made to me about the martyred oligarch, Mikhail Khodorkovsky: 'The mistake he made was to forget what country he was living in.'

One of the conditions of Ai Weiwei's release was that he not talk to the media. There has also been a clampdown on speech in the aftermath of the Salakhova affair. Azerbaijan's authoritarian power structure has made frank debate over the president's decision impossible within the country. Salakhova issued a statement that her works had been removed because of 'certain technical problems which occurred during the transport of the items', with no mention of censorship: a very Soviet kind of explanation. A little later, in the semi-privacy of her Facebook page, she linked without comment to multiple articles that accurately described the censorship of the works but attributed it to the Azerbaijan Ministry of Culture. The curator of the pavilion, Beral Madra, also issued a statement blaming the censorship on the Ministry of Culture, with no mention of a personal decision by the president. The Ministry of Culture itself blandly referred to 'damage to two sculptures during their transport to Venice'. The natural conclusion is that both artist and curator, and indeed the Ministry of Culture, have been intimidated, directly or indirectly, by the power of the president himself. Salakhova is from an elite Azerbaijani family and presumably they depend in some measure on Aliev's goodwill in order to prosper.

This absence of discussion is crucial. Art is not only things, it is the discourse around them. There is in the end no artistic freedom without broader freedom of speech, because the art object is entwined with the words that contextualise it and has no independent intellectual existence. So the expansion of contemporary art around the world presupposes tolerance, not only of all sorts of imagery and objects, but also of their immanent ideological content, all the words they potentially provoke. This is not just a rights issue, it has implications for art. If discussion is not allowed, art is denatured; it degrades to a matter of craftsmanship and aesthetic decision-making which reflect the superficial but not the profound attributes of art in the western tradition. Whatever the commercial success, the art made in these new territories may turn out to lie outside, not inside, the mainstream of contemporary art.

What is sometimes called the Judaeo-Christian tradition is of course better adapted to the consequences of the *filioque*: it *gave* us the *filioque*. But even here historical divergence from it is palpable. The Orthodox

Church, after a brief reconciliation at the Council of Florence in 1439, eventually turned down the *filioque* and Russia has, as a consequence, a troubled relationship with the visual art of the]West, which it accepted only in the 18th century (for Russian censorship of art, see my earlier essay for *Index on Censorship*, 'Shut The Duck Up', Volume 3, 1/2008). And in the West, although naked bodies are okay by the churches, the post-Romantic occupation of pseudo-spiritual space by artists has brought art and religion into regular conflict. Artists arrogate to themselves the privilege of ethical analysis and this inevitably rubs up against the sphere of influence of Christianity.

In 2010, after complaints from the Catholic League and Representative John Boehner, the Smithsonian National Portrait Gallery in Washington, DC, removed David Wojnarowicz's film, *A Fire in My Belly*, which featured such Bunuelian imagery as ants crawling over a crucifix, from the exhibition *Hide/Seek: Difference and Desire in American Portraiture.* Andres Serrano's 'Piss Christ', the photograph of a plastic crucifix in a bath of the artist's urine and blood, was exhibited in Avignon in 2010, where it faced a protest campaign launched by Catholic movements. Even John Berger, author of one of the classic texts of contemporary art, *Ways of Seeing*, weighed in: in the French press he objected to the work's title, which he described as an act of aggression. On Palm Sunday it was attacked and damaged by a hammer-wielding visitor. No mistake by Berger. Both works, Wojnarowicz's and Serrano's, *are* in fact acts of aggression, and directed specifically against the Catholic Church. They have their origin in their authors' horror at the Aids epidemic and are polemical against the Catholic Church's indifferent attitude to the suffering arising from it.

The surrender of spiritual authority is almost complete

These are important but definitely localised hostilities, concerned with the proper attitude to a minority group. When it comes to Christianity, even fundamentalist Christianity, the truth of the matter is that the game is up. The surrender of spiritual authority by the Christian church to art is, in my opinion, almost complete, despite little flare-ups of dissent. Art is our new spirituality: where else do people go on Sunday in London except to the Tate or Maureen Paley's Interim Art? More than that, it is our new ideology. The US State Department ultimately chooses who will represent the United States at the Venice Biennale. The US pavilion, according to David Mees, the US cultural attaché in Rome, quoted in the *New York Times*, is a tool of foreign policy, something the administration refers to as 'soft diplomacy'. When, say, the British Council takes a work by Barbara Hepworth to Iran, it is installing the relic of an alternative belief system just as the early Christians replaced pagan idols with body parts of the saints. This is not a uniquely Anglo-American perception of the uses of art to shape global consciousness. Today, Ukraine's Viktor Pinchuk buys works by Damien Hirst and Jeff Koons by the dozen and commissions an art museum in Kiev with a specific intent: to bind Ukraine to the West and separate it from Russia. Another post-Soviet oligarch, Vyacheslav Kantor, has opened a Museum of Avant-Garde Mastery in Geneva. Its collection consists mostly of works by Russian-Jewish artists. The museum (I quote the website) is 'an integral part of an international programme called the Jewish Positioning System (JPS), which was created to influence public opinion about Jews using positive examples and focusing on their contributions to society and the country'.

Which brings us to the Judaeo in Judaeo-Christian. Eugenio Merino's work 'Stairway to Heaven', exhibited at the ARCO art fair in Madrid in 2010, shows three religious figures praying atop one another. Each prays in a characteristic pose. The Muslim is doubled over, face to the ground; a Catholic priest kneels upright on the Muslim's back; and a Hassid stands on the Christian's shoulders. If that sounds like one of those jokes that begins something like 'There was a rabbi, a priest and an imam ...', well, maybe it is one of those jokes. Be that as it may, the Israeli Embassy in Madrid denounced the work as 'offensive to Jews, Israelis and probably others' and accused Merino of hiding behind the mantra of freedom of expression. Merino responded by describing 'Stairway to Heaven' as a reflection of the 'alliance of civilisations' all in the service of God.

There was, in fact, no big kerfuffle around 'Stairway to Heaven'. The Israeli Embassy protested but, mindful of the accusation that it might be seen to be attempting censorship, did not ask for the work to be withdrawn, and it stayed in place. It was a footnote in the history of censorship, almost a non-event. Perhaps it wasn't an attempt at censorship at all, just an indication of dismay. However, it is interesting to consider the case of 'Stairway to Heaven' because it illuminates matters not covered in

Eugenio Merino, 'Stairway to Heaven'
Courtesy: the artist

עץ חיים
ETZ HAYIM

the discussion above. One is the business of the representation of things Judaic/Jewish/Israeli. The other is the nature of the contemporary art object which, although it is an object embedded in discourse, is not finally definable by any discourse. It allows multiple interpretations: what else for the instrument of PLT?

The ambassador objected to a work depicting a number of religious figures on behalf of a nation-state, Israel, and a people, the Jews (in fact the ambassador's complaint didn't specify an insult to Judaism at all). The complaint, then, reflected a specific assumption of the essential identity of these three categories: the Judaic, the Jewish and the Israeli. It's a specific assumption because one cannot imagine it in relation to a sculpture of, say, a priest of the Church of England, which would probably not be interpreted, even by a British ambassador, as automatically representing (a) the English and (b) the geo-political entity called England. This difference reflects the different histories of different people, places and religions – the history of the Jews is not the history of the English – and it's not my intention to analyse how far the ambassador's assumption about Judaism is borne out by the reality. The trouble here, from the point of view of freedom of expression, is that the ambassador's elision of categories would tend to transform any criticism, satire or ridicule of the institution of Judaism into a form of anti-Semitism. So, considering the sanctions in our society against racial or ethnic disparagement, his complaint does perhaps amount to a form of attempted censorship; it is at the very least implicit encouragement for others to come forward and censor. Israeli diplomatic sources reported that 'the term "anti-Semitic" was deliberately avoided, for fear of provoking a wave of anti-Jewish and anti-Israeli feeling in Spain', but in fact the insinuation of anti-Semitism is patent. That's a loaded charge in the world of contemporary art, which has a large and influential Jewish contingent, and could curtail an artist's career.

Of course, maybe Merino's sculpture is not merely a bit of fun poked at religious types but truly anti-Semitic. An objection in my mind to the ambassador's complaint is that he doesn't specify the nature of the insult contained in the work. But I suppose he might argue that the figures in Merino's work are symbolic of a whole culture, not of specific religious adherence, and the implication of the sculpture is that this is the World Order: Jews on top, standing on everyone else and crushing them down. Is that a legitimate reading? Yes, at least ever since Dr Seuss's *Yertle the Turtle*, which presents a similar scenario: a pile of turtles, with the king on top and poor Yertle at the bottom (in the end, Yertle pulls himself free and the whole tower collapses). What do I actually think about the piece? I was struck not by the possible symbolism of anti-Semitism, maybe because all the Jews I know are non-observant, but by the implicit history of prayer: the more recent the religion, the more self-abasing the obeisance, as though the newcomers felt they had to try harder. But I wouldn't want to privilege my reading over the ambassador's or anyone else's: again, it is a given of any significant work of contemporary art that it is capable of multiple readings. The task of contemporary art is to stimulate the imagination, not shut it down. I suspect that, the process of creation being what it is, Merino was struck by the possibility of stacking those three modes one on the other: the work is a kind of apt visual joke from which we can extract whatever meaning we want. I hazard a guess that he went ahead with the work *despite* the potential charge of anti-Semitism, of which he must have been conscious, but not because of it. That may not suit the Israeli ambassador, but it's surely Merino's prerogative as an artist; in fact, as an activist in the church of PLT, it's his duty to do whatever he likes without fear or favour. In the end, 'Stairway to Heaven' was bought by a Jewish collector in Belgium. ❒

40(3): 57/73
DOI 10.1177/0306422011418437
www.indexoncensorship.org

Matthew Bown is the proprietor of the Matthew Bown Gallery. He is the author of several books about Russian art as well as the documentary film *My Night with Julia*

PICTURE THIS

Eugenio Merino on 'Piss Christ' by Andres Serrano

Many works of art have influenced the way in which I work. I am interested in those that break through artistic barriers and directly touch the heart of society: works that subvert the system and attempt to find the cracks within it.

The first piece that had a real impact on me was Andres Serrano's 1987 'Piss Christ', a photograph that I saw for the first time when I was studying at the Bellas Artes in Madrid. It was censored when it first appeared, and Andres Serrano received numerous death threats. What is interesting is that the piece is extremely beautiful and its meaning only becomes completely clear when the title is read. What generally happens with such works is that the creator's comments have little weight as the censors have already taken their decision and leave no room for doubt. We live in a society that is adopting the ideology of the politically correct and are becoming wary of expressing ourselves for fear of causing offence. Euphemism has become established as a way of repressing ideas, and the meaning of things is becoming diluted. For this reason, beauty is not enough. Art should not be a pleasant, beautiful escape mechanism. It should not be a euphemism covering over the holes in society, but the light that makes us reflect upon that society. That is why art is and will always be uncomfortable for the system. Art must move closer to activism rather than to the purely aesthetic. There is no aesthetic without ethics.

In 'Piss Christ', Andres Serrano casts doubt on belief and purity. And it is this doubt which 'offends', since religion is based on dogma and absolute certainty. This year, the piece was attacked in the Contemporary Art Museum in Avignon and slashed beyond recovery by a number of Catholic demonstrators. This is a violent, anti-democratic stance, typical of totalitarian groups that only allow a single vision of the world. Absolute certainty.

Andres Serrano's 'Piss Christ'
Credit: photo by Jean-Paul Pelissier/Reuters

The freedom to create and express oneself is a right that places obstacles in the path of the censorship of artistic expression or at least legitimises our desire to work without restrictions. This means that we are not in the service of anything or anyone, neither religion, politics nor society. We are only motivated by our ideas and convictions, and it is this that makes art something more than a beautiful object. All this is why artists such as Andres Serrano, Ai Weiwei, Mauricio Cattelan, Jota Castro, Santiago Sierra, Marc Bijl and Democracia are so important. Not because they make sculptures, paintings or installations, but because each of them wakes us up and alerts us to what is hidden behind the scenes. ❒

Translated by Christina MacSweeney
40(3): 74/76
DOI: 10.1177/0306422011418427
www.indexoncensorship.org

Eugenio Merino is an artist based in Madrid, Spain. His works include '4 the love of go(l)d' (2009) and 'Stairway to Heaven' (2010), both of which met with controversy when exhibited at Madrid's ARCO fair

A warning to the ruling military council and interim cabinet, post-revolution graffiti
Credit: 3arabawy

ART OR VANDALISM?

Street art has become one of the symbols of freedom in Cairo. **Yasmine El Rashidi** reports

Ayman handed himself in at noon on 27 April 2009. The police had been searching for him for three days, and his name had made headlines in the local press. He was the criminal still at large – his two accomplices had already been caught. They were held in an unknown location, under investigation. We all knew they were being interrogated, maybe even tortured.

The phone call had come the night before.

'We need your help.'

'They're looking for him.'

'He's scared to go alone.'

'I'm not sure what to do. Nobody wants to touch this case. I need you on this one, can you go with him?'

Ayman was a friend and I had worked with him on projects in the past. Maybe the presence of a woman would lessen the brutality he might face.

The police seemed surprised when we showed up the following day. In Mubarak's Egypt, the police and state security were known for their heinous torture methods and arbitrary detentions. Nobody voluntarily handed themselves in, and we weren't sure what they would do. Ayman admitted he was sick from fear. That morning, his face was drawn and he was gnawing at his nails.

At the downtown police station – a decrepit villa that had long ago been seized from a family who was forced to flee – we were escorted up worn stairs to a pre-fab top floor. There, in a cramped, smoky room, we were left to wait. I was offered a chair, Ayman the floor. He chose to stand.

Over the hours as we waited, mid-ranking officers came to ask who we were, what our case was.

'I'm an artist,' Ayman would say. 'I make art.'

'She helps me come up with ideas.'

We had rehearsed our narrative: I was the ideas person – the one who came up with the project. He just executed – made the art. We had prepared a paper – the 'project proposal' to give our story legitimacy, to try to break down the project in a language the police could understand. Our document began (in Arabic): 'Inspired by the rise of street art around the world, and the growing emphasis being placed globally on the artist as community activist, Cairo-based artist Ayman took to the streets of Cairo last month in an effort to use his art to contribute to the city.'

The officers trailed in over the course of four hours. Each asked a question or two before nodding their heads and leaving. They seemed ill-equipped

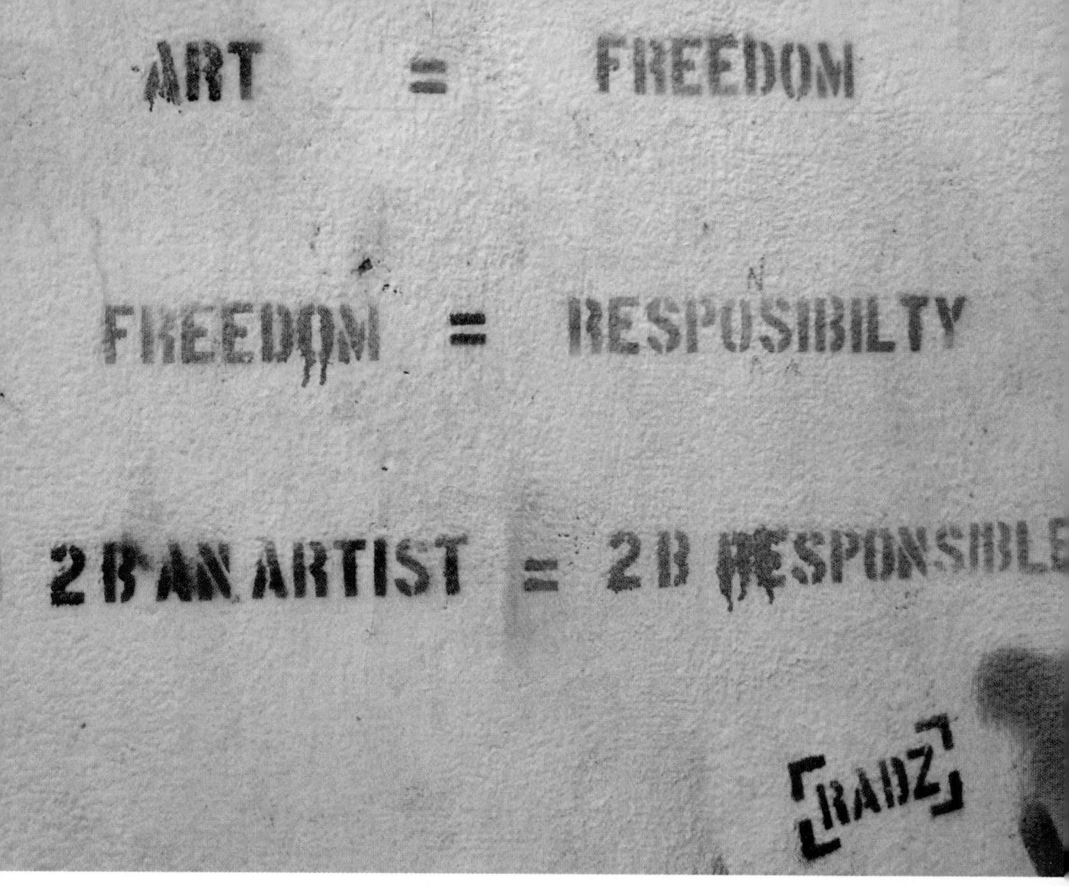

Post-revolution graffiti
Credit: Yasmine El Rashidi

to deal with our case, and eventually, we were told that we would have to wait for the top-ranking officer – the head of the police station – to arrive. He didn't come in to work before late afternoon, but we could go in there. They pointed to another room with a rusty iron bed and flattened sponge mattress.

'There's a TV on,' an officer told us.

'Enjoy,' he added, as he walked out laughing at the screaming blaring from the TV – a torture scene in an underground Egyptian jail. An Egyptian thriller and drama.

Ayman was formally detained later that night. Over 14 hours, we had been subjected to endless rounds of questioning by police, a trip to a nearby court, and three interrogations by high-ranking officers; they already seemed to know everything about us, but each quizzically took us in, unsure what to conclude.

At 2am, they told me I could leave. Ayman, they said, would have to wait. He would spend the night in the police station jail. The charges were

A noose with the word 'retribution' written beneath it, post-revolution graffiti
Credit: Yasmine El Rashidi

yet unknown. The police were unsure how to classify his act: what it meant, how great a danger he may be.

'It looks like it could be the eagle on the Egyptian flag with its wing broken,' we had heard one officer say in the hours as we waited. 'Maybe that means, destroy the government.'

'It is a communist movement,' another offered.

'They want to overthrow the regime,' an informant said.

That night in the police station, Ayman stayed up, pacing. He was to be transferred to the state security headquarters early the following morning for further interrogation. At 7am the prison truck would arrive, the officer had told me before I left. 'You can wait for him outside,' he said. 'But we don't know how long it will take. You might be there for days.'

In the next 48 hours, waiting for Ayman's release, I learnt the police side of the story. They woke up one morning, one of them told me, and found

Protesters accused the government of buying tear gas from the US, post-revolution graffiti
Credit: Yasmine El Rashidi

five streets surrounding Tahrir Square filled with a 'strange looking' figure painted on the walls. 'It looked like it might have been a cult,' one officer told me. 'Definitely a threat to the government.'

'One young officer ignored the first of these paintings, but then, the next morning, there were so many more of them. We couldn't ignore it. We weren't really sure what it was. The idea of writing on walls being art makes no sense to us.'

The graffiti on the streets downtown for which Ayman had been arrested depicted a street sweeper. A thin stencil outline of a man holding a broom. 'Keep your city clean' was the thought behind his abstract art, 'Love your country.'

One of them admitted: 'None of the officers want to sign off on his case. No one is really sure how many followers he has and what this is really about. What does this symbol really mean? What is the message? We can't take the risk. No one wants to lose their jobs.'

Street sweeper by Ayman Ramadan
Courtesy the artist

I met up with Ayman again on 28 June 2011, on a sidestreet near Tahrir Square, just minutes from where his street art had once been and around the corner from the state security headquarters where he had been blindfolded and interrogated. Clashes between protesters and riot police had begun late the night before, and by the morning, the street was the site of a pitched battle. Protestors chanted against the military, some of them threw rocks. The riot police responded with rounds of tear gas.

For hours this battle went on – the protesters moving forward, the police firing back. Young men and women were being carried out of the crowds, hit by tear-gas canisters or faint from the gas. A young boy went up in flames. There were informants in our midst, and soldiers in the distance, but the crowd relentlessly pushed on – not willing to yield.

During the 18 days of the Egyptian revolution, when the police were symbolically defeated and the army took control of the streets and the state, our fears of the notorious state security apparatus had been broken, and the streets of our cities had become, in many ways, our own.

'I feel I can do whatever I want now,' a friend had told me soon after Mubarak stepped down. 'I want to spray the streets with paint.'

In the weeks that followed, my friend, other friends, artists, non-artists, took to the streets to do just that: fill the walls of the streets of Cairo with murals and art. 'Freedom = Responsibility', paintings of the martyrs, 'VIVA EGYPT', abstract collages of the Egyptian flag, pastiches of symbols of liberation. The self-censorship that we had all long subjected ourselves to was slowly lifting. The signs of it were everywhere.

Our fears had been broken. The streets had become our own

Last week, on that sidestreet of Tahrir, by a graffiti scrawl that said 'F*** the Police', Ayman and I talked about how things had changed.

'We're free now,' he said as he snapped pictures on his phone. 'We can do whatever we want.'

'New: Freedom Mask, courtesy the Supreme Council of Armed Forces' by Ganzeer
Courtesy the artist

قناع الحرية

تحية من المجلس الأعلى للقوات المسلحة
إلى أبناء الوطن الحبيب

حاليا بالأسواق ولفترة غير محدودة

Some weeks ago, a friend and artist, MoFa, also known as Ganzeer, organised a 'mad graffiti weekend' intended to 'take back' the streets of the city. For many days he and a group of activists, artists, friends and volunteers gathered in his rooftop studio to discuss their plans.

By the time they hit the streets mid-May, they had stencils ready, vast supplies of paint, walls identified, and friends to photograph and film them. Their graffiti largely mocked and criticised the ruling military council, which had risen to power since Mubarak stepped down on 11 February. It depicted the underwear of the ruling Field Marshall Mohamed Hussein Tantawi, 'freedom masks', or muzzles, that spoke of the reality of military rule, and murals of army helicopters and life-size tanks.

MoFa, along with some friends, made posters of one of the works – the Freedom Muzzle, criticising Field Marshall Tantawi. On 25 May, as they were plastering the poster downtown ahead of a big protest planned for that weekend, MoFa and two friends were detained – to be released, quite swiftly, several hours later after straightforward questioning.

I received an email the next day when the news hit the local press.

'I'm sure you've seen this,' my friend Bruce – an international critic, a dean at the American University in Cairo, and big supporter of street art – wrote, referencing a link to an article about the arrests.

I wrote back: 'I do. But I'm not sure how much sympathy I have. Around the world street art is considered vandalism, so content aside, this should come as no surprise. When Ayman was arrested a few years ago, no one was willing to support him. Of course now all these guys are raging about how bad the army is. Yes, the army is problematic, but, in the military council's mind, it's these same youth who were burning the Israeli flag and threatening to storm the embassy last week. That was one of the most destructive acts to the legacy of this revolution – to its peaceful nature, to its spirit. Why not use street art to raise awareness, to subtly provoke thought, to reach out to the masses? Are direct political statements art? Is provoking animosity towards the army art?'

Some weeks later, on the one-year anniversary of the death of Khaled Said, the 28-year-old man who was beaten to death at the hands of police last year, activists and citizens at large took to the streets in his memory. Many of them held up pictures of him. Others hoisted the Egyptian flag. Some had stencils and cans of paint – portraits of Khaled that were plastered on downtown streets: on random buildings, on the walls of the Ministry of Interior, on shop windows and shutters. One of the portraits was sprayed over the marble plaque of the American University's Rare Books

Portrait of Khaled Said
Courtesy Pierre Sioufi

AMERICAN UNIVERSITY

RARE BOOKS AND SPECIAL COLLECTIONS LIBRARY

ارحل يا عيسوى

and Special Collections Library, which stands a few blocks from Tahrir. A friend took a picture of it. I sent it to Bruce. 'Art or vandalism?' I wrote in the subject line. ❐

40(3): 78/88
DOI 10.1177/0306422011418583
www.indexoncensorship.org

Yasmine El Rashidi is a writer based in Cairo. She is a frequent contributor to the *New York Review of Books* and the author of *The Battle for Egypt: Dispatches from the Revolution* (New York Review of Books)

RUSSIA'S ROBIN HOOD

Widespread frustration with the establishment has fostered a brand of political street art that's taking the country by storm. **Nick Sturdee** reports

Scandal goes down well in the art world, and the organisers of this April's prestigious state Innovation art award in Moscow clearly decided to make the most of their moment. The queues outside the cavernous Garage Centre for Contemporary Culture – Konstantin Melnikov's 1927 constructivist bus depot refurbished as a gallery for Dasha Zhukova, Roman Abramovich's wife, and graced by Amy Winehouse at its opening in 2008 – were to be expected; so of course were the chic crowd and the TV cameras. But the on-stage video installation of revolution in Cairo, Japanese tsunami, and London student riots – accompanied by epic dissonant swells and jabbing chords, lyrics shouted by a male voice choir and an albino's falsetto solo – was an unmistakable statement. We live in momentous times, Russia is no exception (or hopes not to be) and Russian art is ready for the challenge.

The Innovation jury had resisted attempts by officials and bureaucrats to block the nomination of 'Cock held captive by the FSB', an explosive 2010 action by the street art group Voina ('War'). Two of its performers had only recently been released from jail. Five artists had painted a 60-metre tall phallus on Liteinyi Bridge in St Petersburg just before it was raised to stand erect above the city's security headquarters – the KGB/FSB building central to Vladimir Putin's life story – to allow for ships to pass all night long. It was a veritable two fingers up to the security apparatus so pre-eminent and seemingly ubiquitous in Putin's Russia.

As the Innovation jury head Andrei Erofeev pronounced Voina winner of the visual art category, there was no concealing the triumph on his face. A long-time combatant of art censorship in Russia, his exhibition of banned art had itself been closed and he had been fined. Erofeev had championed Voina. He asked the audience if they dared name the piece by its real name (in the programme the expletive 'cock' had been replaced by 'member'), and the correct version was duly shouted back in unison by a delighted crowd. The Moscow art world was enjoying a moment of strange carnivalesque liberation, for old-time dissidents and young artists alike. And yet in the fashionable bar afterwards, a group of businessmen denied all knowledge of the group when I asked them to comment on camera and a young gallery owner declined to explain why people might take pleasure in the FSB being insulted. 'I have a career to think of,' she said. 'Big brother is everywhere.' Evidently what I had witnessed was a battle won, not a war.

War on the street

Voina's action had been brilliantly planned and executed, it was refreshingly low-tech and delightfully accessible. Over two weeks of clandestine observation, the group calculated they had an average of just 30 seconds between traffic being stopped and Liteinyi Bridge being raised for the night. Over the same two weeks they practised daily with water in a parking lot, dividing the phallus into five 'cuts' with one artist responsible for each, and perfecting the assembly of the five cuts into a well-formed and recognisable whole, completed within the 30 seconds. Fifty-five litres of white water-based emulsion paint mixed with water were divided into five-litre canisters, two together for the penis head and testicles in order to achieve the required thickness. Further activists distracted the bridge security in their roles of drunken football fan, nervy woman driver and cyclists. On the night, the group stormed the bridge and completed the phallus in 23 seconds; the only blemish a slightly ill-formed left testicle due to one of the artists being taken out by a security guard. An incredulous crowd wondered and photographed as the bridge towered insolently above the FSB headquarters.

Soon the Voina group followed up their action with another performance, overturning seven empty police cars one September night in St Petersburg. Again, all was meticulously planned and executed with aplomb: five

Orgy staged by Voina at the Moscow Biological Museum on the eve of presidential elections, February 2008
Credit: Voina Group

activists overturned each car – taking an average of nine seconds – while, when required, others distracted local police by pretending to be foreign tourists needing help. On completion, the group posted a film on YouTube called 'Palace Coup' ('coup' in Russian is the same word as 'overturn' and 'palace' from the same root as 'yard', where the cars were overturned). The video began with a small boy (Kasper, the son of two members of Voina, Oleg Vorotnikov and Natalia Sokol, aka Koza) playing football in a St Petersburg park. The boy kicks the ball out of shot, and in the next shot the ball rolls under a police car parked at night outside a police station. Five figures cross the road and overturn the car, and at the end of the video one of the figures (Leonid Nikolaev) returns the ball to Koza as she holds Kasper in her arms. In case anyone had missed the point, Nikolaev – the third key member of the group – released a statement: 'I helped the child – and I will help the country!'

The Palace Coup was the culmination of some four years of relentless political art and actions by Voina, designed to challenge the viewer and mock the Russian authorities and law. Oleg Vorotnikov says the aims are still wider: to demonstrate to people that they should not be scared of the authorities. Some performances are political and lifestyle statements that enact plays on words, thus apparently drawing from Russian conceptualist art. 'Fuck for the heir the Little Bear!' was an orgy displayed by the group at the Moscow Biological Museum at the end of February 2008, on the eve of Dmitry Medvedev's election as president, where the election was portrayed as a ritual of copulation in order to greet Putin's anointed successor, whose name derives from 'medved', Russian for 'bear'. 'How to steal a chicken', in July 2010, showed a Voina activist in a shop doing just that, by concealing it up her vagina (a verb from the Russian slang for vagina means 'to steal'). The action demonstrated Voina's lifestyle principle of not paying for food, thus not recognising, and 'fucking', the 'thieving Russian economy and authorities that are destroying the Russian people'.

Other performances have been more straightforward and more directly aimed at the police and other groups charged with upholding law and morality in Russia. In July 2008, Vorotnikov dressed up as an Orthodox priest with a policeman's hat, entered a supermarket, filled a trolley full of food and left without paying. In November the same year, Voina commemorated the October Revolution by staging 'The Storming of the White House': a huge anarchist skull and crossbones were projected on the national government building, the White House, and scenes from Sergei Eisenstein's film *October* were re-enacted by scaling the complex's towering gates. (In *October*, it was the Winter Palace that was stormed.) In May 2010, Nikolaev mounted a car belonging to a Kremlin security official with a blue traffic cone on his head to protest at the impunity with which officials are perceived to behave in Russia. (This was during a wider protest movement at bureaucrats' abuse of privileges by using emergency lanes while the rest of the population had to stand in traffic. The bureaucrats' cars have blue flashing lights on top.)

While there has been some debate in art circles as to whether their actions constitute art or not, the group see themselves as artists with a social duty. Sitting in a St Petersburg burger joint at midnight while deciding where he, Koza and Kasper would spend the night, Vorotnikov told me that it was his duty as an artist to express openly what other people fear to express, to offend the police, and thus protect the people 'like Robin Hood'. The words – expressed with a slight flash of irony in

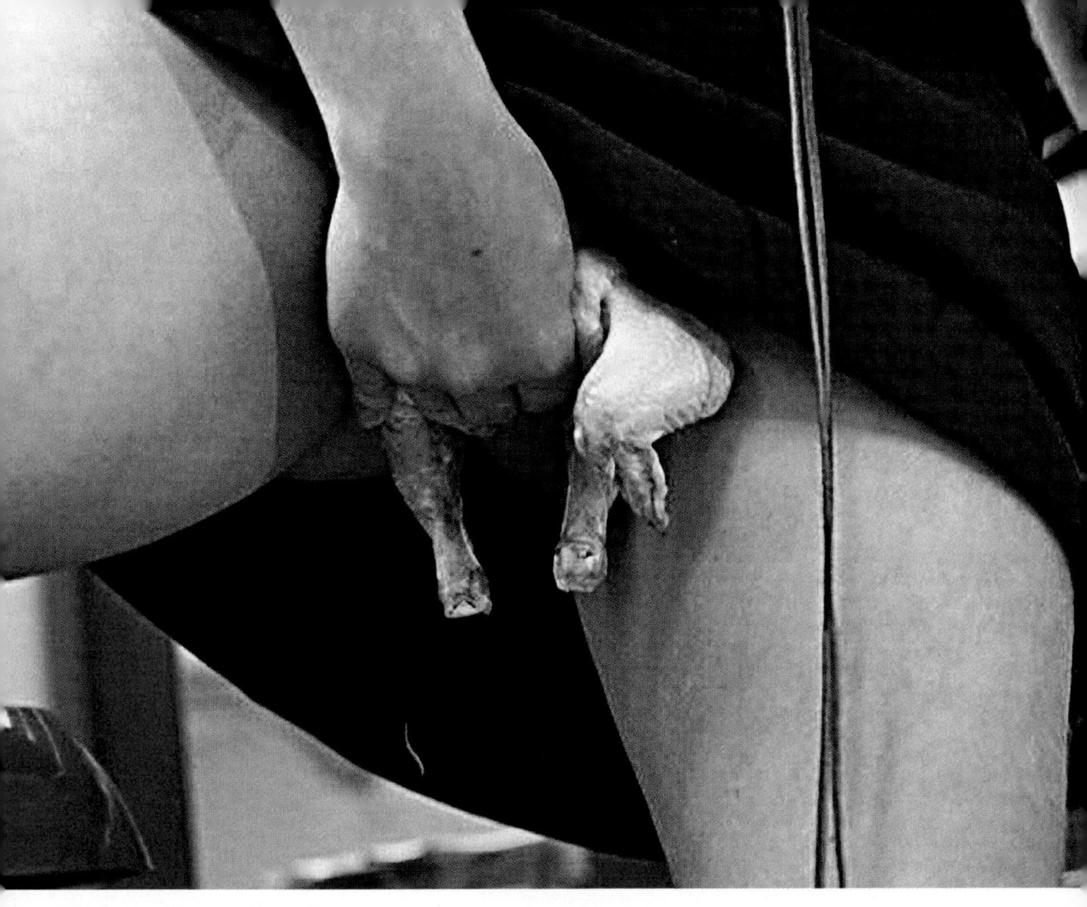

Still from Voina's How to Steal a Chicken
Credit: Voina Group

Oleg's eyes – replay a time-honoured tradition of Russian intellectuals and artists. He then resumed his social-network planning for the next day on his laptop: Voina is certainly a remixed version of the St Petersburg narrative – and one that has won its place on the international map of street art, or 'art terrorists', as the group's admirer Banksy put it. And it's not the only tradition into which Voina inscribe themselves. Sitting in another cafe (the group lead an itinerant lifestyle and keep no mobile phones in order to evade police surveillance), Oleg discussed his time in prison with the veteran political activist and prisoner Maxim Gromov from the National Bolshevik Party. It was almost quaint, a repeat of conversations that must have been held a hundred years ago in similar cafes in the same city, by revolutionaries of a bygone age. It smacked of the Soviet prison legacy: over 80 people in one cell, sharing beds and sleeping in rotation, one hole in the floor for everyone's needs. Only the details were more modern. Imagine having the bunk next to that, I thought.

The whole Voina lifestyle and narrative are something of a performance; it is about public self-representation, certainly. This is part of what makes them artists, say their supporters. But naturally the police are not to be distracted by such arguments, and when the group overturned the seven police cars, it was decided that it was clearly time for the security forces to play their part. In November 2010, Vorotnikov and Nikolaev were duly arrested in a raid by the Extremism Police – a special police unit active on most towns in Russia – on the flat where they were staying in Moscow. Handcuffed and laid on the floor of a minibus for the ten-hour drive to St Petersburg, Vorotnikov and Nikolaev were then charged with 'aggravated hooliganism' and 'incitement of hatred of a social group' (the police) and held in a pre-trial detention prison. The pair were freed on bail after three months, following a campaign both in Russia and elsewhere – Banksy raised some £80,000 (US$127,738) to pay for lawyers, bail and to support the group's further activity. Days later, the Innovation award nominations were announced.

Political art on the map

When Voina made the shortlist for the visual art category of Innovation, it was evidently a major embarrassment for the authorities. After the nomination there followed a treadmill of rumour and behind-the-scenes pressure. First of all it was claimed that the group had not consented to the nomination. Then the entry was excluded on the grounds that documentation was lacking or late. Finally, the Ministry of Culture attempted to bypass the award's jury and leave the decision to the far more conservative 'organisational committee'. When the jury complained, nominated artists threatened to drop out and publicity became too great, the Voina nomination remained. Then pressure on the jury began in order at least to prevent the bridge from winning: it would be fine for the action to win for purely aesthetic reasons, argued officials, but it would be improper for a piece of art to win that appealed to people's political views.

When Voina duly won at Innovation, Russia's Public Chamber – a 'civil society' body created by the Putin machine – demanded the award be retracted. The body decried the use of public funds on an award that was a 'slap in the face of common sense' and those who saw the 'image on the bridge' as 'banal hooliganism'. But the horse had clearly bolted – and even the Culture Ministry, itself rebuked by the Chamber for not preventing the result, stated that it would respect the jury's decision.

Police escort Voina member Leonid Nikolaev to his hearing, 14 January 2011
Credit: Alexei Danichev/Ria Novosti/Camera Press

The Innovation episode – trivial though it may seem – was a crucial battle in the freedom of artistic expression in Russia that most in the art community felt needed to be won. Not everyone liked the Voina action: some artists and critics compared it unfavourably with similar but more ironic performances in the 90s, some saw it as a 'symptom' of the mood in Russia rather than something more meaningful, a more accomplished, more 'mature' work. Others were uncomfortable with art whose effect derived from political emotion as much as aesthetic response.

Political expression had irreversibly entered the artistic establishment

Yet in the face of the state's attempt to interfere with the prize, jury members put aside their aesthetic reservations and awarded Voina the prize. As the critic Ekaterina Degot put it, 'It would have been improper not to'. Political expression had thus irreversibly entered the artistic establishment and political art had been defended as a legitimate form of expression.

This recognition was also welcomed by those who felt that the flourishing art scene in Russia was beginning to police itself too closely. Some considered that since the 90s big money and strong galleries were threatening to stifle the scope of artistic expression by 'academising' what was art and excluding what was not. Political art was needed and was capable of generating immense resonance in a country where contempt for bureaucrats and corrupt officials in all walks of life – not least security – seems to be becoming universal. Commenting on her support for Voina, Degot described how Voina expressed a feeling in society of historic proportion: 'The hatred for United Russia [Putin's party] and for the authorities in general has reached a level comparable only with the hatred for the communists in 1988. That hatred is at boiling point, eating up people inside and – unlike 1988 – it has no constitutional expression. That hatred is Voina, it is a powerful symptom that is impossible to ignore. When they see the bridge, for them it is like looking at an icon ... Humiliated, intimidated, and stripped of their rights, citizens look at Voina's phallus in the internet like a protective icon ... Voina is art, and not something else. Voina does not exist in the political sphere – but instead of politics.'

Voina's 'Cock held captive by the FSB', 2010
Credit: Voina Group

Supporters of curator Andrei Erofeev hold a poster that reads 'Down with censorship! Honour the artist!', Moscow, May 2008. He was charged with incitement of religious enmity in 2007
Credit: Denis Sinyakov/Reuters

The bigger picture

While Voina has been the most successful – and most controversial – exponent of art 'instead of politics', the group is not alone. Novosibirsk artist Artem Loskutov has for two years organised absurdist street demonstrations called 'Monstrations', where hundreds of participants march with apparently meaningless signs (such as 'Yyyt', 'Chunga-Changa', 'Why are you so nervous?' and 'Tanya, don't cry!'). The effect is a carnivalesque subversion of politics and plays on the lack of dialogue in the political scene in Russia. Ilya Falkovskii, Aleksei Katalkin and Boris Spiridonov and their music and animation group PG Dreli post playfully menacing videos on the internet – such as young men firing a bazooka at Vladimir Putin's motorcade – and photographs such as 'Somalia is Here' (with armed militants firing on government buildings in Moscow). Grigory Yushchenko exhibited a series of traditional 'lubok' pictures of drunken policemen in a Siberian art gallery, while the group 'Sinie

Nosy' ('Blue Noses') produces satirical prints, the most famous of which – 'The Era of Mercy' – depicts two Russian policemen kissing tenderly in a snow-covered birch forest.

Then there are activists and bloggers whose activity is categorised as politics but whose style and self-representation are not far from those of many of the artists listed – and certainly not far from Innovation laureates Voina. Underground political activity and the internet are saturated with such content. The 'revolutionary socialist' DSPA (Petr Alekseev Resistance Movement) – are friends of Voina and have a history of unfurling banners satirising and mocking the St Petersburg and national leadership, often with deliberately childlike word play. The National Bolshevik Party, a kind of post-modern revolutionary party created and led by the writer Eduard Limonov, has aligned and realigned itself with various strands of nationalist and anarchist thought, and is adept at being at the forefront of street protest. The musician Savva Terentyev, who wrote in his much-quoted phrase in his Live Journal blog that one or preferably two policemen should be burned in the central square every day, has become a well-known counter-culture figure. Flash mobs abound, and periodically mass protest groups emerge and form around a single issue – such as hundreds of car owners and YouTube users in the 'blue-bucket' campaigns against bureaucrats abusing privilege to use emergency lanes on Moscow's congested streets.

Artists and activists are targeted with the same legislation

Not only can it be difficult for observers and journalists to define a difference between art and political activism. In recent years artists and activists in the growing political underground in Russia have increasingly been targeted with the same legislation. A raft of laws have been used: most notoriously, two articles in the Russian Criminal Code, 282 and 213, both ostensibly designed to protect society and religious and social groups from 'incitement of hatred' and 'hooliganism', have been deployed increasingly often against artists and political activists. This has been facilitated by the importance the Russian executive and legislative authorities have afforded anti-extremist legislation – to which Article 282 is related – that has been developed and bolstered since 2002. Critics complain that the wording of legislation is vague, thus allowing the police and security services to wield the same legislation against Islamist terrorists, neo-Nazi gangs, anarchist groups, bloggers and artists. Other laws, such as 'insulting a representative of the authorities' (Article 319), and breaking the 'official use of state symbols' (Article 17.10 in the Administrative Code) – in other words, misusing the Russian flag – have also been cited.

An important case occurred in spring 2008, when curators Andrei Erofeev and Yury Samorudov were charged under Article 282 with the incitement of religious enmity for their 2006 exhibition *Forbidden Art*, which had shown pieces of art that had been recently banned – mostly for their questioning of or mocking stance on religion. Prosecutors sought a three-year prison sentence, but the two men were just fined. Erofeev then lost his job as contemporary art curator at the Tretyakov Gallery. At about the same time, observers began to notice a tendency for the phrase 'social group' – which Articles 282 and 213 both list as potential victims of a crime – to be applied to various arms of the state and its security apparatus. The musician and blogger Savva Terentyev was arrested and subsequently given a suspended sentence for 'inciting hatred' of the police as a social group in his blog, also under Article 282. In 2009, Artem Loskutov was called in for questioning by the local Extremism Police just before holding the May 'Monstratsia'. He was cautioned against conducting the action and, after ignoring the warnings and another invitation to chat, was later stopped by police who he claims planted marijuana on him. At the trial it emerged that the Extremism Police had been wiretapping his phone. In December 2010, he was once again detained, and as a result has now been charged under another law, Article 319 – insulting a representative of the authorities. Allegedly he made offensive remarks to a police officer on duty – on the occasion that he claims the drugs were planted. He was also accused of being offensive in his online account of a night spent in a police cell, in which he caricatured a policeman. The trial started in June.

PG Dreli, a politically active group, fell victims to a security forces clear-up in streets near the Kremlin, where they had managed to find a studio. Ironically, it seems that these anti-fascist activists lost their prime location partly as a result of nationalist and racist riots near the Kremlin in December. According to other artists who also lost their studios, the Kremlin security outfit was carrying out a full reconnaissance of the area in the wake of the violence. When they entered PG Dreli's studio, they were shocked to discover artwork such as a series of photographs of guerrillas taking pot-shots with bazookas at key buildings in Moscow (including the FSB headquarters, the Lubyanka). The security personnel are also reported to have seen 'Vampire', a video the group made depicting a man plotting to attack Putin's motorcade as he stood, bazooka in hand, next to the very window from which the studio looked onto the Kremlin. One imagines the Kremlin security outfit found it hard to appreciate the art they were beholding. The property developer owning the building was instructed to remove PG Dreli from the studio (he also evicted the other artists from their studios for good measure). Security guards met one of the suspected artists, Ilya Falkovsky, as he arrived to clear his stuff out. During the course of a long nocturnal discussion, agents allegedly threatened Falkovsky with violence and to plant drugs or weapons on him in order to ensure a lengthy jail sentence; they also asked whether he would like to act as an informer on 'extremists' he knew. Falkovsky left the country for – of all places – China (where his wife is from).

This bizarre story illustrates the deeply problematic gulf between artists and Russia's security services. Naturally, where anti-extremism police may fear real action, Russia's political artists' work is symbolic. For critics like Ekaterina Degot, this is proof that the artists are actors of the aesthetic rather than political sphere. And yet, in an atmosphere of increasing radicalisation and alienation among young people in Russia, the concerns and action of the authorities may even make their fears closer to reality. As I sat with Voina in a St Petersburg burger bar, they were discussing their lives since their release. The prison experience, continued attention from the Extremism Police (who seem to survey the group), and the threat of real prison sentences following criminal charges, leave decreasing time for art performance. They are spending considerable time, and the money they have received from Banksy and from the Innovation award, on their legal struggle and on supporting others they see as facing persecution from the authorities. As Oleg Vorotnikov says, 'Banksy is bankrolling the next Russian revolution – and I think he'd be pleased.'

The group see themselves as artists – but Oleg says that for him the ethical is ultimately more important than the aesthetic. We watch a video of a recent political demonstration in which they participated, and it is striking that their activity appears to be moving closer to pure direct action. The video shows the members preparing bottles of urine before the demonstration – in case of a confrontation with the police. When they are prevented from blocking a road, and Leonid Nikolaev is targeted and dragged away by the police, they spray the police with the urine they have prepared. Oleg's explanation of the event concentrates on the symbolic: the urine is physically harmless, but according to the prison subculture in which the police and much of Russian society are steeped, the police have been deeply and profoundly humiliated. I'm not sure this is so specific to Russia and to its criminal lore, but there is no doubt that the event is far stronger, and indeed more interesting and more capable of generating meaning, as symbolic art – rather than as a potentially fringe and slightly pitiful political act.

The incident only added to Voina's problems. In July, a court ordered Vorotnikov's arrest for failing to obey bail terms. In addition to the original charge under Article 213 (hooliganism and incitement of hatred against a social group), he also faces charges under Articles 318 (using violence against a representative of the authorities) and 319 (insulting a representative of the authorities). Now officially a wanted man, he is currently in hiding. The group also say they are concerned by threats that have been made by members of the Extremism Police over the right to custody of their child, Kasper.

Voina are now apparently staying in a basement with no running water and say that the demonstration was not one of their performances. Indeed, it seems they have not been able to enact one since their release from jail. But now they appear to be preparing for something new. 'We have been preparing a very powerful and daring plan for two months now', they write. 'It will be a wonder-action. We have little strength, we are cornered by the police on all sides, but our ambitions are beast-like. The result will be something very joyful and very frightening! But very harmonious.' It will be interesting to see what this extraordinary group comes up with. Russian political street art is certainly on the move, and the parliamentary and presidential elections over the next six months might well provide a good stage. ❐

40(3): 89/102
DOI 10.1177/0306422011418758
www.indexoncensorship.org

Nick Sturdee is a filmmaker, producer and writer. His films include *Stolen Brides* and *Chechnya's Missing Women*. He is currently making a film about Voina

ART UNDER FIRE

A timeline of censorship in the name of decency, from Aubrey Beardsley to Richard Prince

1966

A **Gustav Metzger** exhibition is raided in London and the artist is charged with putting on an 'indecent exhibition'; the following year the courts fine him £100.

London police remove a stock of **Aubrey Beardsley** post-cards from a shop in Regent Street, referring to them as 'obscene prints'.

Works by **Jim Dine** and **Eduardo Paolozzi** are confiscated from London's Robert Fraser Gallery; Fraser is charged under the Obscene Publications Act of 1959. Dine's work is found to be indecent but 'not obscene', and Fraser is fined 20 guineas.

1969

US customs agents in Baltimore confiscate works by **Hans Bellmer, George Grosz, Karel Appel, Melle** and **Cesare Peverelli** en route from Europe for an exhibition.

Artist Jim Dine, 1977
Credit: Lewinski Archive at Chatsworth/Bridgeman Art Library

The artworks include explicit images of male and female genitalia and are banned under federal laws prohibiting import. Later, both the trial court and the Fourth Circuit Court of Appeals find that the works all have artistic value, and are therefore not legally 'obscene'.

1970s **Jacqueline Livingston** is fired from her position as a photography professor at Cornell University and charged with possessing child pornography. She had taken photos of her son masturbating and close-ups of her husband's and father-in-law's genitals. The case was dismissed in the 1980s.

1988 **Sally Mann**'s book *At Twelve: Portraits of Young Women* provokes controversy due to its depictions of adolescent girls.

1989 A photography exhibition by **Robert Mapplethorpe** at the Institute of Contemporary Art (ICA), Philadelphia, leads to a lengthy court case in which the Cincinnati Contemporary Arts Center and its director are charged with exhibiting pornography. The exhibition is cancelled by the Corcoran Gallery of Art, Washington DC, and Congress declares the ICA ineligible for National Endowment for the Art (NEA) grants for five years.

1990 **Judy Chicago**'s 'The Dinner Party' (1979) is donated to the University of District of Columbia, but is withdrawn after Congressman Robert K Dornan refers to it as 'ceramic 3-D pornography'.

1992 **Sally Mann**'s photography book *Immediate Family* causes widespread controversy. The *Wall Street Journal* censors one of the book's photographs, 'Virginia at 4', covering up the subject's eyes, nipples and pubic area.

1996 Indian artist **Maqbool Fida Husain** faces obscenity charges following the publication of an article about his depiction of Hindu deities in the nude. The paintings, which were produced in the 1970s, led to outrage among some conservative Hindu communities. In 2008, the Supreme Court acquits Husain just before his 93rd birthday.

Pontiac, Michigan, lodges obscenity charges against Detroit artist **Jef Bourgeau**. His exhibition *Art Until Now* had been 'postponed' by officials at the Detroit Institute of Arts the previous year. The opening of the 2000 exhibit coincides with a public forum on art and censorship. Charges against him are dropped in June.

2001 Police attempt to remove photographs by **Tierney Gearon** from the *I am a Camera* exhibition at London's Saatchi Gallery. Gearon's photographs of her children naked are branded 'pornographic' and 'revolting' by a tabloid and fine art publisher Edward Booth-Clibborn is given an ultimatum to remove thousands of copies of the accompanying exhibition catalogue he published.

Detail of 'The Dinner Party' by Judy Chicago, 1979
Credit: AFP/Getty Images

Joel-Peter Witkin's 'Maquette for Crucifix', depicting a naked Christ surrounded by sadomasochistic imagery, creates widespread controversy and again invites criticism about artistic projects funded by taxpayer's money.

For the first time in its 200-year history, **Christie's** auction house has to issue a warning in one of its catalogues over the sexual content of some of the images for sale. Scotland Yard's obscene publications squad investigates explicit images by **Wolfgang Tillmans**, **Richard Prince**, and **Andres Serrano**.

2003

'Obscene paintings' by **DH Lawrence**, banned in 1929 when originally displayed at London's Warren Gallery, go on show at Waterstone's bookshop in Piccadilly. The

Robert Mapplethorpe, 'Ajitto', 1981, gelatine silver print
Credit: Bridgeman Art Library

Obscenity and the law

The *Protection of Children Act* (1978) is the most relevant law governing the indecent representation of children in the UK. The law states that it is an offence to possess and display 'indecent' photographs or pseudo-photographs of a child under the age of 16. Public indecency can also be charged under the *Obscene Publications Act* (1959), the *Indecent Displays (Control) Act* (1959) and the common law offence of outraging public decency.

The first thing the prosecution team would need to prove to a jury is that the photographs of the children are 'indecent'. UK courts stipulate it cannot be indecent to depict naked children in cases where a photograph contains no sexual overtones (*Commissioners of Customs and Excise v Sun and Health*, 1973). The decision played a key role in the DPP's decision not to prosecute the Saatchi Gallery for exhibiting photographs by Tierney Gearon in 2001. The works featured her own young children naked, and included the controversial photograph of her five-year-old son urinating into snow.

Furthermore, a gallery or museum director would usually have recourse to the special defence that they had a 'legitimate reason' for holding and exhibiting the images in question. A claim of 'artistic expression' offers considerable protection to galleries and museums, particularly for photographic images that have long circulated in the public domain.

In the unlikely event that a gallery's directors were eventually convicted under the act, they would still have recourse to appeal to the European Court of Human Rights. This is because any such conviction in the UK would be likely to infringe Article 10 – the right to freedom of expression – as guaranteed under the European Convention on Human Rights. *Daniel McClean.*

A version of this article was originally published on frieze.com on 10 October 2010
40(3): 103/112
DOI 10.1177/0306422011418906
www.indexoncensorship.org

Daniel McClean is a lawyer specialising in art, media and intellectual property and is the editor of *The Trials of Art* (Ridinghouse)

M F Husain at Pundole Art Gallery, Mumbai, India
Credit: Dinodia Photos/Alamy

original ban technically remains in place, but police say they are 'unlikely' to take action unless they receive complaints.

2005 A triptych by **Francis Bacon** showing two men lying on a bed with 'attendants' is briefly displayed in Iran's Museum of Contemporary Art before being removed by Basij militia during the exhibition's first day. The painting is part of a collection owned by Farah Pahlavi, the late Shah's wife; her Renoir portrait of a semi-nude girl is not included in the exhibit.

2007 In Gujarat, student **Chandra Mohan** is arrested after his paintings are deemed 'obscene' because they feature male nudes; his work is also vandalised. The dean of the

I Am a Camera, *Saatchi Gallery, featuring photographs from Tierney Gearon's* Untitled *series*
Credit: Richard Stonehouse/Camera Press

arts faculty at the university is suspended for opposing the student's arrest.

2008

Police seize photographs of naked adolescents by critically acclaimed artist **Bill Henson** in May. After seizing 21 out of 40 artworks from an exhibition at Sydney's Roslyn Oxley9 Gallery on 23 May, three more of Henson's photographs were removed from the Albury Regional Art Gallery in New South Wales. Authorities announced plans to charge Henson under the Child Protection Act, but these were later dropped after it emerged that the images were not in breach of the law. In June, the country's Classification Board ruled that Henson's art was suitable for general release, including on websites.

2009

Kathleen Neill, a 26-year-old life model, is arrested at New York's Metropolitan Museum of Art for posing naked for a photographer in full view of visitors.

A photograph by **Richard Prince** is removed from the Tate Modern's exhibition *Pop Life: Art in a Material World*. The Metropolitan Police advised the gallery to remove the photograph, which features actress Brooke Shields aged ten posing in the nude, arguing that the gallery could be in breach of the law by allowing the work to be shown. Much of the photographer's work involves rephotographing the work of others and this image, 'Spiritual America', is a photograph of an original by Gary Gross taken in 1976.

A US comic book collector pleads guilty to importing and distributing **Japanese manga books** that feature illustrations of child sex and bestiality.

2010

Curators at the poster museum in Aarhus, Denmark, cancel a retrospective by art group **Surrend** due to open in October after a new poster is submitted for display. The museum's director accuses artists Jan Egesborg and Pia Bertelsen of trying to 'attract attention' after being presented with a poster that featured cartoon images of members of the Danish Royal Family in various sexual positions.

Savannah College of Art and Design removes a photograph of a sitting male nude holding and partially covering his genitals photographed by fourth-year student **Nicole Craine**. College administrators say that the content would be 'unacceptable' for a 'family event'.

Authorities at Abu Dhabi airport censor an advertisement in copies of *Le Monde* newspaper after they discover it features a nude painting by **Lucas Cranach**. Sections of 'The Three Graces', promoting a major exhibition at the Paris Louvre Museum, are blacked out with marker pen before going on sale.

2011

In late October, the Toronto Art Fair requests that work by Canadian painter **Andrew Morrow** be shrouded from public view by black curtains and that a sign be displayed alongside it, warning visitors of its explicit sexual nature. Organisers also exclude reproductions of the art from the fair's catalogue, claiming that it interfered with their aim of trying to create a 'family-friendly' environment.

A documentary about Spanish artist **Juan Francisco Casas** is removed from YouTube because it 'violated company policy relating to nudity and sexual content'. The film features photographs of Casas' drawings, many of which contain half-naked subjects.

Facebook pulls the account of New York art curator **Savannah Spirit** after she posts photographs advertising her erotic art show 'Hotter Than July: A Sexploration'. Facebook deems the work sexually explicit. ❒

Sources:
Associated Press, artdesigncafé™, *Art Newspaper,* Artnet, Australianmuseum.net.au, BBC, *Bound and Gagged* by Alan Travis (Profile Books), Asia Society, Cafe Babel, Censorship in America, *Copenhagen Post,* the *Guardian*, the *Independent*, Kennethafriedman.com, the *Los Angeles Times*, *Ottawa Citizen, Soho Journal, Sydney Morning Herald*, the *Telegraph*, Thomas Jefferson Center, *The Times*, *Toronto Life,* Wired.com

Due to the trial of Faryadi Sarwar Zardad currently in progress at the Old Bailey, this work has been removed temporarily following legal advice.

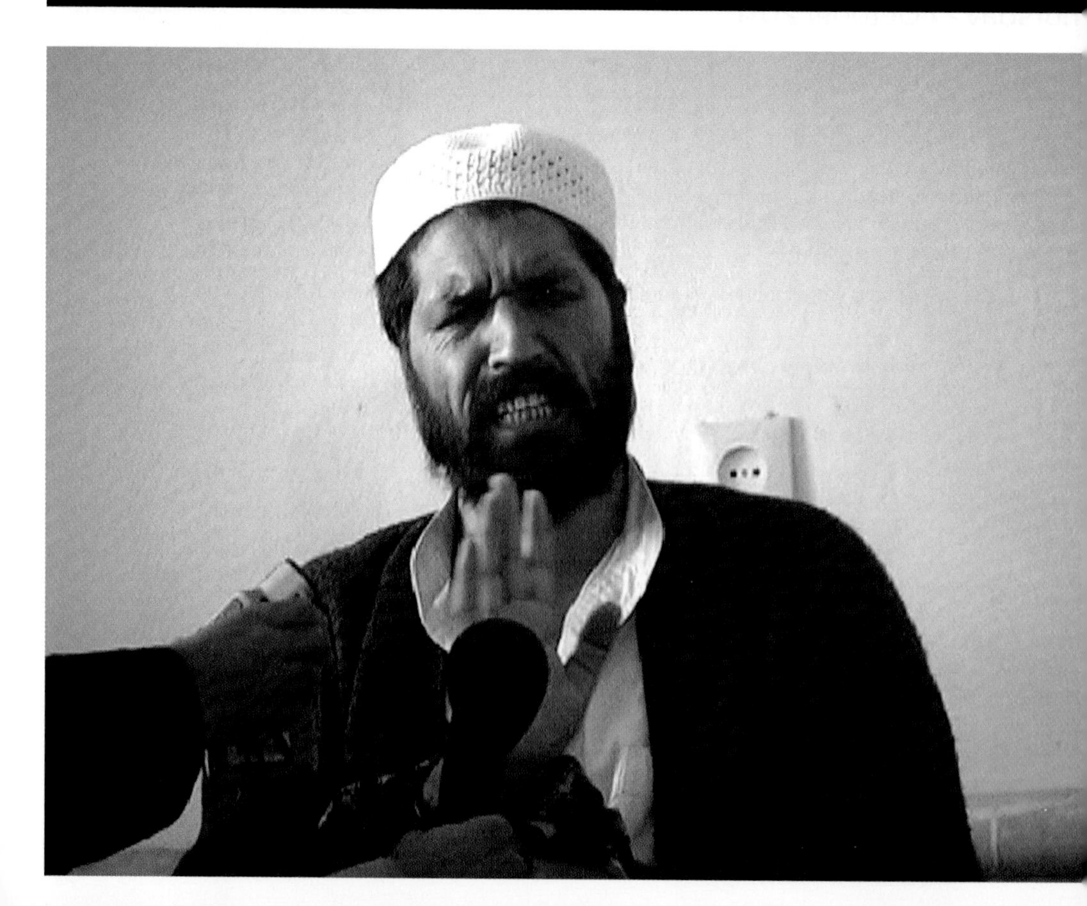

PICTURE THIS

Langlands & Bell on 'The House of Osama bin Laden'

We were shortlisted by Tate as candidates for the 2004 Turner Prize for an artwork titled 'The House of Osama bin Laden', a trilogy of video and interactive digital artworks made following a research visit to Afghanistan as 'war artists' in 2002. The core artwork in the trilogy is an interactive digital reconstruction of the former house of Osama bin Laden at Daruntah in eastern Afghanistan that allows viewers to use a joystick console to virtually explore the compound he once occupied.

The other two artworks in the trilogy are 'NGO', a dual screen digital animation exploring the role of the NGOs and disaster relief agencies that were engaged in 'reconstructing' the country at the time, and 'Zardad's Dog', a film we shot at the Supreme Court in Kabul during the first capital trial after the fall of the Taliban. The defendant in the trial was Abdullah Shah, a vicious local fighter employed by the ruthless 'Commander' Zardad in the Sarobi area east of Kabul during the civil war of the late 90s. Shah was known notoriously as 'Zardad's Dog' because he was kept on a chain in a cave and reputedly used by Zardad to terrorise locals and those in transit on the main road from Kabul to Peshawar by savaging the testicles of victims with his teeth. When the Taliban came to power, Commander Zardad fled to Britain to avoid persecution and was given asylum, while Shah was arrested and held in prison in Afghanistan. Following the trial that we recorded at the Supreme Court, Shah was returned to Kabul's Pul-i-Charki prison and shot dead in extrajudicial circumstances, which were criticised by Amnesty International at the time.

Newsnight first broadcast Zardad's presence in London on 26 July 2000 when the Taliban's foreign minister in Kabul, Wakil Ahmed Muttawakil, retorted during an interview with correspondent John Simpson, 'Well, you British are sheltering the criminal Commander Zardad.' As a result, Zardad, who had been living in Streatham and running a pizza parlour in Bexleyheath

Top: The 'legal screen' displayed at the 2004 Turner Prize exhibition at Tate Britain. Although the text states that the work was 'temporarily' removed, the work was not reinstated during the run of the show. Zardad's Dog *was shown at the Tate Britain on its own a year later, but not in the intended context of the original exhibition*
Bottom: still from Zardad's Dog

for three years, was arrested and bailed by the Metropolitan Police on several occasions before finally being brought to trial at the Old Bailey for torture and hostage-taking.

Unfortunately, the date of Zardad's trial at the Old Bailey coincided with our presentation for the Turner Prize at Tate Britain. A few days before the opening of the exhibition, we were suddenly informed by Tate's curators that we would not be permitted to show our film *Zardad's Dog* (which constituted a third of our presentation) for fear of Tate being considered to be in contempt of court. Because Tate failed to provide us with more information but still insisted on us withdrawing the film, we sought the advice of the lawyer Hugh Tomlinson QC. Tomlinson advised that if we removed direct reference to Zardad from the film's inter-titles (black screens that occur briefly within the flow of moving imagery to offer explanation of the narrative) and modified the title of the film slightly – for example by substituting the word 'human' for the word 'Zardad's' in the film's title, calling it instead *Human Dog* – it would be extremely unlikely that Tate could be considered to be in contempt of court. Tomlinson advised us that these precautions applied equally to our book *The House of Osama bin Laden*, simultaneously being published by Thames & Hudson. Unfortunately, although Thames & Hudson were reassured by Tomlinson's advice and published the book, Tate refused to accept it and insisted again on us removing the film from the exhibition. Tate then also removed the Thames & Hudson book from display on the desk of artist publications in the exhibition's ancillary reading room, despite all references to Commander Zardad having been blacked out or substituted as recommended by Tomlinson.

We had been reluctant to withdraw from the exhibition altogether for several reasons: after protracted negotiation we were allowed to display a notice in the exhibition explaining that part of our work had been withdrawn for legal reasons; 2004 was the last year in which we qualified as potential candidates for the Turner Prize due to the age ban on those aged 50 or over being eligible; we were assured by the curators that despite the removal of the film from public exhibition, the Turner Prize judges would still be shown the film at full scale within our installation as we had originally intended it to be seen by visitors to the exhibition. We later discovered that this didn't happen; we were told that the judges watched the film crowded around a laptop instead. In the end, we had little confidence in Tate being fully transparent about the reasons or the circumstances surrounding the removal of the work. Viewed in retrospect, our decision not to withdraw from the exhibition at Tate entirely may have been a mistake.

However, because the artwork is so relevant, there has been continued interest in it and we have continued to exhibit 'The House of Osama bin Laden' Works from this trilogy have now been seen in 15 museums and galleries in ten different countries around the world. ❐

40(3): 114/117
DOI: 10.1177/0306422011419126
www.indexoncensorship.org

Ben Langlands & Nikki Bell have been collaborating since 1978 and have exhibited on an international basis since the early 80s. Their art ranges from film and digital media projects to sculpture, installation and full-scale architecture

SPACES OF FREEDOM

Shaheen Merali talks to **Rozita Sharafjahan**, artist and director of the pioneering Azad Gallery in Tehran about pushing the boundaries

Shaheen Merali: Tell me about the history of the Azad Gallery.

Rozita Sharafjahan: Thirty-five years ago, as a teenager, art was an extracurricular activity. I then went on to art school, before college. This was at the time of the 1979 revolution. What has stayed the same in my relationship with art, through all these experiences, is the idea of resistance, the aspects of dispute and remaining critical.

My career in art began within the education system, or more specifically my career in painting did, which was never a medium of choice for me but rather a way out of the limitations of the art school curriculum. After finishing high school, the universities were closed. The cultural revolution meant that they remained closed – to rid them of western cultural influence.

There was a repressive atmosphere for intellectuals over the next two years. So we artists and intellectuals were inhibited from the start. The situation continued for 20 years after the revolution and was exacerbated during the [Iran–Iraq] war, putting additional restraints on intellectuals and artists. By the time [Mohammad] Khatami had risen to prominence [president of Iran

Untitled, shredded photograph, 2011
Courtesy Katayoun Karami

1997–2005] and there was a clearer space for intellectuals, we were able to mature and move past the constraints and fears in society.

We were concerned that all connections and relationships were easily broken in such a repressive atmosphere. So the idea of a gallery came about as a way of breaking out of this isolation, to find people we could work with. And it's been very effective in bringing people back together. Gradually, newer generations have grown to love the Azad Gallery and have come to see it as an intimate space for conversation, free from the political and economic issues that limit the discussion of art. I believe the success of the gallery today owes much to an audacious culture that explores radical ideas within art and welcomes a new generation [of artists].

Shaheen Merali: Would you please comment on the current state of restlessness in the country?

Rozita Sharafjahan: Iran – and other countries in a similar situation – has faced government repression over a long period. This has resulted in mounting frustration for the population as a whole. It has also created an almost hysterical desire within Iranians; each generation pursues these desires, only to be frustrated. Disillusionment then sets in and it is left to the next generation to take up the baton. What is even more important is the build-up of greed and desire that causes such hysteria. You can witness this hysteria in many exhibitions, by examining the artworks: they tend to be very busy, using a wide range of ideas and media.

Shaheen Merali: So, in this idea of the 'hysterical desire', there seem to be two main issues affecting artistic production for artists living and working in Iran: economic sanctions and the power of the censor. Would you please describe their impact on individual artists' work?

Rozita Sharafjahan: I think it is too soon to pass judgment on the effect of the sanctions. For a short period after the revolution, we had to face these economic sanctions and they had a very detrimental effect on the arts. Artists faced a virtual boycott, cut off from the rest of the world, in a very restricted space. Nowadays it seems boycotting contemporary Iranian artists is no longer possible.

Art and culture in Iran have been facing censorship for the past 100 years – this is not a new phenomenon. Circumventing censorship seems to have become inexorably entwined with Iranian art. For example, the

Parastou Forouhar , Sombulist 20; Sombulist 18; Sombulist 2
Courtesy: Azad Gallery/the artist

language that has been developed and embedded in our culture is highly metaphorical and, in a sense, artists avoid being direct; they don't express their feelings straightforwardly.

The new generation has been able to free itself from using metaphorical language, but this is a small group compared to those who still use this way of 'dressing' reality. I believe the biggest issue is religion, rather than politics. This is basically entrenched in our society: it is this, rather than government repression, that forces us to censor ourselves.

Shaheen Merali: What has been the impact of this on the creative sector in the last decade?

Rozita Sharafjahan: I think that the main question here is how far defiant forms of art can have a political impact. As someone who runs a gallery, I thought it was my job to push the boundaries. I think artists have come to understand that the red lines are not fixed, and with defiance and resistance you can push them further. In the past 12 years, at different exhibitions, people have wondered how we got away with showing some of the art works on display. Nothing has stopped us from pursuing our work; we've had some small issues with the government over the years here and there but they never resulted in shutting down the gallery. This demonstrates, quite obviously, that fears come from within, rather than from outside.

Shaheen Merali: How does censorship affect the Azad Gallery? And how does the gallery plan for the future in light of continuing tensions between artists and the authorities? Is there a strategy in place?

Rozita Sharafjahan: We don't have any direct relationship with the authorities. The stronger and more powerful we become, the more the pressure from the Ministry of Culture diminishes. One element of this strength is fame, which helps secure the gallery's space. For example, the artist Parastou Forouhar is well known and so has more room for manoeuvre than many other artists. When we decided to put on an exhibition of hers in 2009 at the gallery, nobody believed the exhibition would complete its full run. I heard (and still hear through students) of people knowing about the show but not daring to come. This is a form of negotiating with power. Political experience tells you that it will not end in disaster with government intervention. Shahab Fatouhi's show (*Val'Adiata Zabhaa*) last year even transformed the gallery into a presidential campaign centre for the [former] candidate Mir Hossein

Moussavi. After the turmoil of the 2009 election, even our neighbours wondered how that show didn't get the gallery into trouble.

There are a few more cases like these. What I mean to say is that we don't undertake the task of mediating between the arts and the authorities, but still push boundaries.

Shaheen Merali: Do you think artists living and working in Iran are creating a new sense of aesthetics which allows them to speak with layered meanings and/or in poetic terms?

Rozita Sharafjahan: No, this isn't what's happening right now, quite the contrary in fact. I believe the new generation has been distancing itself from this tendency. The new generation has been exposed to western art and this has allowed them to be more direct and frank.

Shaheen Merali: The new generation of artists who produce so much, some of whom graduated in the last decade, have been profoundly affected by the recent political instability in Iran. Can you describe their methods, concentrating on specific subjects and the ways that make them different from the previous generation?

Rozita Sharafjahan: One specific theme more visible in the new generation is that of sexuality. I believe this is a cultural issue rather than a political one. So far, it seems that the new generation has shown more courage and audacity in breaking down cultural taboos in this area.

Shaheen Merali: By being more explicit, more daring?

Rozita Sharafjahan: They are not only more explicit. The fact that they even attempt to deal with such issues, which were almost absent in the work of my generation, which was even more silent than [previous generations], shows great daring.

Sexuality was not considered sublime enough to occupy any space in art and, at the same time, if artists wanted to talk about sexuality, they were never able to be explicit about it; women remained almost completely silent and men focused on aesthetics to turn it into something that appeared sublime.

Shaheen Merali: And gay politics in general?

Rozita Sharafjahan: As I said before, the earlier generations and the one before mine were absolutely silent on this – it is the new generation that is paying attention to these issues. The theme has become predominant among artists who have emigrated from Iran, like Ramin Haerizadeh and Behrouz Raie.

Shaheen Merali: What do you envisage for the future of artistic production and the public space in Tehran and Iran?

Rozita Sharafjahan: I think our biggest problem is the disconnection between our art and the public arena. We know that if we want to be more powerful – in the sense of finding the strength to resist censorship – we need to connect with and be present in the public sphere. It seems to me that the government is well aware of this situation, and this is evident in their attempt to keep art confined to gallery space. A lot of the shows we put on display we believe to be very audacious, and yet there are no obvious consequences as a result. Nothing happens; we are both [co-director Mohsen Nabizadeh] happy we did not face any consequences but also sad and deeply aware that there is a disconnection, highlighted by the very limited number of artists and collectors who see the shows.

There was a time when artists were limited to the space of their studios. Now they have realised they need not be confined within such boundaries. It seems that at least the past two generations are aware that they have to break out of their studios and galleries in order to make art in public areas and engage with society at large. For example, artists are not allowed to take photographs or shoot footage on the street; as a result, you need to recreate the social space in your own studio. This creates a sort of artificiality in the artworks and reduces the possibilities of connecting with the audience. A lot of performances that have taken place in the gallery ought really to have been in public spaces; since they are indoors they become pale imitations of what they really should have been. ❐

Translated by Foad Torshizi
Interview conducted in Tehran, 27 June 2011
40(3): 118/125
DOI: 10.1177/0306422011418232
www.indexoncensorship.org

Shaheen Merali is an independent curator and writer based in London. He curated The (Iranian) Weltanschauung at the Freies Gallery Berlin this summer in collaboration with Azad Gallery

Credit: Majid Koorang Beheshti

Strip Search by Martin Rowson
OOH GOODY! I'M FINALLY GOING TO GET THE CHANCE TO SEE THE WORLD'S MOST FAMOUS PAINTING IN THE FLESH...
GUIDE
THIS WAY
2
MOVE MOVE MOVE!!!
WHAT THE?
BLIMEY!
3
GO GO GO!!!
4

5
AHEM! UM... "DEAR CUSTOMER! WE APOLOGISE FOR ANY DISRUPTION TO YOUR VISITOR EXPERIENCE. THIS WAS NECESSITATED BY THE PRIORITY TO ENSURE YOUR SAFETY AND PROTECTION FROM RECENTLY UNCOVERED SUBLIMINAL ATTACKS TO DISSEMINATE ECONOMIC SABOTAGE, MORAL DELINQUENCY, INDECENCY, OBSCENITY AND THE PROMOTION AND GLORIFICATION OF TERRORISM IN CERTAIN ITEMS ON DISPLAY. THIS HAS NOW BEEN CORRECTED. HAVE A NICE DAY!"

FOOL FOR ART

Society needs to protect not only the right to artistic expression, but also the artist's work, regardless of aesthetic value, says **Jude Kelly**

I chaired a conference a while ago in Switzerland about looted art. Interpol and the British police were amongst the participants. It was about the right to protect objects. Curators from Baghdad gave moving evidence in which they described how the museums were invaded by professional looters when war broke out. They even brought diggers in on helicopters, landed them in the desert, drove them to ancient tombs, shot the security guards, dug up the prized objects and then took them to Switzerland and stored them there. The conference revealed that there is no known place, whether it's a body like Unesco or civil laws, that safeguards not only the right to artistic expression but the right to keep that artistic expression protected, on behalf of the people.

At the moment Unesco is trying to pass a law to protect the object for civil society. It's a debate that exposes an ambivalence about whether an object has meaning – and for whom it has meaning. The role of the artist is totally negotiable in society, depending on whether people feel like having him or her around or not.

In a society like ours, we are selling the idea that one of the USPs about the UK is its unique ability to be creative and to turn the light on for many

The 'Lady of Warka' was reinstated at the Baghdad Museum after being found by Iraqi and US forces on 16 September 2003. The 5,000-year-old artefact was looted in the early days of the Iraq war
Credit: Aladin Abdel Naby AN/JV/Reuters

kinds of expression. If, at the same time, we have such an ambivalence about the role of the artist and our right to protect the artist then I think that we have an undernourished conversation in this area. It might be even more endangered, strangely enough, at this particular point in time when democratisation of the arts is something that we are promoting in a very proactive way. There's been huge excitement about the possibility that the audience has moved from being splendid appreciators to being active makers and this has undoubtedly changed the way that art is made, and the conversation between artist and audience. In that change of making and receiving there is the great potential for all of us to understand a lot more about the way that art plays out for us. But it also has the possibility, and you'll see this from the recent furore over Opera North and the cancellation of Lee Hall's opera *Beached* in July, that you can suddenly have the reverse. A school whose pupils were participating in the production objected to references to homosexuality in the libretto. An audience who are now participants, as in the case of the opera, may suddenly say: 'We don't like your script and 300 of us are pulling out because we don't think that young people under the age of ten should discuss homosexuality.'

Do we defend Lee's rights as an author or the participants?

The idea that Lee Hall's opera can be pulled, because the audience-participants feel that they have more sway than the artist, takes us to very vexed places. Are they right because they've become the artist? Imagine if 12 actors walked out of a Caryl Churchill play, where would we sit with that? But if 300 amateur actors walk out of a production or are told to walk out by their parents – whose rights can we defend? Lee's rights as an author? Or the 300 children who are the participants?

When Shakespeare wanted to demonstrate that a society was either benign or had the potential for flexibility, he always employed a fool. Macbeth didn't have a fool. If you had a fool it suggested that you had the capacity for wisdom – even if you weren't choosing to listen to that fool on that occasion or in that period in your life. The fool was somewhere between a

King Lear and the Fool on the heath by Charles Folkard, from The Children's Shakespeare, *1911*
Credit: Mary Evans Picture Library/Alamy

CHARLES
FOLKARD/10.

Freudian analyst and a reductive force, offering compressed versions of the truth. It wasn't Lear who hanged his fool but it was Lear who created a state that eventually, through a disregard for other people's voices, a disregard for democracy, engendered a regime that would hang his fool.

So my question is: we're fine with the celebrity artists and we're fine with the artists who have good reputations, but are we fine with the fool? Are we fine with the artist who might be just taking that poking stick and digging us all in the ribs or maybe even in the eye? Is it something that we're all prepared to defend, regardless of aesthetic? Even I may find myself saying: 'Well, do I think the thing that is being attacked is good or bad in terms of its art or its argument?'

Good or bad is not really the point. It's the right to talk about something, the right to say it and the audience's right to take from it anything they wish. We have to believe in an audience's capacity to hold themselves in an intelligent space; the more you give them the arguments, the more they, and that includes all of us, feel that their maturity is growing. Democracy isn't a fixed state, it's a moving state; it's something that keeps growing and developing sophistication.

A friend of mine, now in his late 60s, was brought up in a concentration camp until he was four. He and his mother were then brought over to Britain when the war ended. He lived a normal life, if you can make that normality happen, and he was an accountant. When his mother was dying, she asked to see him, and said that she needed to tell him something. He was very nervous about this encounter because of what she might be about to reveal to him; he had already had a lot to deal with in his memories and thought she was going to reveal something maybe even more horrific. She said, 'I've got to tell you something.'

He said, 'What is it?'

And she answered, 'You're left-handed.'

'What do you mean?' he asked.

And she said, 'In the camps you could not be left-handed. You couldn't have anything about you that was different. You were left-handed and I had to stop you being left-handed. But I've got to tell you now that you are left-handed.'

So he left the hospital. And he said that even as he walked away from the bed he knew that he was a completely different person. Everything about him: his body, his understanding, everything about him had changed within him. He knew he was a different person. He was a left-handed person.

He went on to be the treasurer of the Royal Society of British Sculptors and spent the rest of his life making extraordinary, passionate pieces of sculpture about the Holocaust. He was an artist.

Not everybody who is left-handed is an artist. If we suppress some part of our self or some part of society, some fundamental expression of who we are, then we'll forget. So I think we should be grateful for the artists who remind us that we need our left hand and that, even though the left hand may do something that is left field, actually, where would we be without it? ❐

40(3): 128/133
DOI 10.1177/0306422011418294
www.indexoncensorship.org

Jude Kelly is artistic director of the Southbank Centre. This is an edited version of a keynote speech delivered at the Index on Censorship conference *Beyond Belief* on 5 July 2011

SKETCHES OF DISSENT

Artists in Turkey may face prosecution and even violence, but the contemporary scene is thriving. **Kaya Genç** talks to two generations of iconoclasts

'It was like a punch in the back, I thought some boxer the size of Muhammad Ali was hitting me for a joke. A moment later I felt the cold Rambo-like knife slicing its way through my bowels. Someone had just stabbed me.' Bedri Baykam, once Turkey's most famous artist and still a household name, was describing an attempt on his life last April. Baykam was stabbed after giving a speech at a protest to an audience of locals, activists and journalists in the well-heeled Akatlar district in Istanbul. He had been asked to talk alongside Mehmet Aksoy, sculptor of the famous Statue of Humanity in Kars which portrayed two figures reaching out to each other in an effort to shake hands – a gesture supposedly symbolising the future course of relations between Armenians and Turks. However, a few months after the Turkish Prime Minister Recep Tayyip Erdoğan labelled it 'a freakish statue', the local government decided to demolish the 30-metre construction. The statue was of such massive proportions that people in Armenia could see it from the capital Yerevan.

'My intended killer thought I would collapse after his attack so that he could easily slash my throat,' Baykam says. 'But I stood my ground. He

'A Female Despot', spray paint on polyester, 95 × 95 × 230 cm, 2010
Courtesy: Extrastruggle and Galeri NON

missed my aorta by three millimetres. In my belly was an extra layer of fat, which seems to have saved me. A total miracle really.' A 36-year-old man later surrendered to the police, claiming he was simply 'pissed off with Baykam'.

Baykam was the 'wonder boy' of Turkish painting. My mother, an artist, was a huge fan. I grew up on his paintings and was familiar with his reputation for controversy. So it was an exciting moment when Baykam showed me some of the fine drawings he created as a child prodigy: a set of cartoonish cowboys in perspective, ghostly ballerinas, mythical birds, sensuous nudes and a Picasso-style beggar strolling down the Champs-Élysées, all completed when he was five. Baykam had his first exhibitions at the age of six in Geneva and Bern. In his studio are carefully preserved press clippings from newspapers such as the *Washington Post*, marvelling at the gifts of this *jeune Turc*.

The son of Suphi Baykam, a doctor and leftist minister of the People's Republican Party, Bedri unabashedly likens his own genius to the early success of Mozart. Towards the end of his teenage years he left Istanbul for Paris, where he studied at the Sorbonne and began a renewed, energetic artistic career that centred on conceptual works and paintings aiming to provoke the establishment. He talks passionately about Deniz Gezmiş, the leading figure of the Turkish communist movement, who featured in his paintings; Bedri combined newspaper headings, strong colours and photographs of the political demonstrations that left indelible marks on the chaotic history of the republic.

I consider the stabbing to be an award that praises my politics

During the era immediately following the 1980 coup, Baykam put on shows mocking the military junta. On one occasion, he constructed a device that 'measured' obscenity by analysing the content of the art work placed inside it; he also created a mechanism for burning books. After studying at California College of the Arts, he returned to Turkey full of new ideas. His 'action-painting show' with female models wrestling nude in a nightclub

'We have made a fool out of ourselves in the eyes of the world', photograph, newspaper and painting, 132 x 177cm
Credit: Bedri Baykam

proved to be a definitive event for Turkey's art scene. During the opening of one of his shows in 2005, he herded a flock of sheep into one of the most famous galleries in Istanbul, relishing an insult aimed not only at the politicians who blindly followed the dictates of the generals, but also at curators and the art world.

'Actually, I'd been expecting this kind of physical attack for the last 25 years. I consider the stabbing to be an award that praises my politics,' Baykam says with a sneer on the word 'award', as we continue to walk between the massive canvases in his studio in Beyoğlu. Now in his mid-50s, Baykam is no longer the most radical figure of Istanbul's burgeoning contemporary art scene; in fact, some believe his politics to be regressive. Although his paintings have now been canonised in Istanbul's Museum of Modern Art, one does not come across Baykam's name in the new wave of galleries and experimental spaces for art in the Beyoğlu district where a new, more subtle sensibility seems to be on the rise. A group of this younger generation is associated with the small gallery NON, strategically located on Boğazkesen, the street that stretches from the vibrant Taksim district to Istanbul's Museum of Modern Art. The gallery houses video installations, sketches, notebooks and paintings; every new exhibition there is eagerly awaited in artistic circles and by the younger generation of collectors.

I met its owner Derya Demir, the charismatic daughter of a Turkish father and an English mother, a day after her return from Art Basel. In 2008, Demir and her friend, the Turkish artist Leyla Gediz, curated an exhibition, *The Bitch is Sleeping*, which focused on various fetishistic items, places and concepts that defined life in Istanbul. A year later, following the success of this show, Demir rented a new building in Tophane that would eventually take the name NON.

Compared to the late 90s and the first years of the noughties, when she was a teenager working for various galleries in Istanbul, Demir finds today's art scene more varied and nuanced. She mentions Hale Tenger and Halil Altındere from the younger generation as examples of the pioneering emancipatory approach in Turkish contemporary art; Tenger's 'I Know People Like This' in 1992 consisted of numerous sets of the 'three wise monkeys', arranged in such a way that the installation formed a crescent amidst stars – with an obvious echo of the Turkish flag. Tenger was accused of violating the notorious penal code of the country and later acquitted. Altındere made headlines when a photograph in an exhibition he curated for the Istanbul Biennial in 2005 – depicting a guard facing a civilian concealing a bottle behind his back – was taken as an insult to the armed forces; he was also prosecuted and acquitted.

When asked to define the distinct characteristics of the new generation of young artists, Demir points to their interdisciplinary, non-academic attitude to art. 'These artists are not specifically focused on just one medium, many of them did not have a formal education in the visual arts,' she says. Although extremely proud of contemporary artists' cultural impact, Demir seems reluctant to talk about their politics. She is understandably weary of political interviews following an attack on her gallery last year.

Demir had planned simultaneous openings with three other galleries in order to welcome last year's autumn art season. As her guests left that evening they were approached by 50 men armed with batons, broken bottles and even a gas bomb; the mob attacked NON while Demir desperately tried to bring down the gallery shutters in an effort to protect those

2009 Baskı
T.C. ANAYASASI
Hakları Evrensel Beyannamesi
Hakları Avrupa Sözleşmesi
Hukuk Cep Kitapları Dizisinin Diğer Kitapları İçin Yayınevimizden Bilgi İsteyiniz.

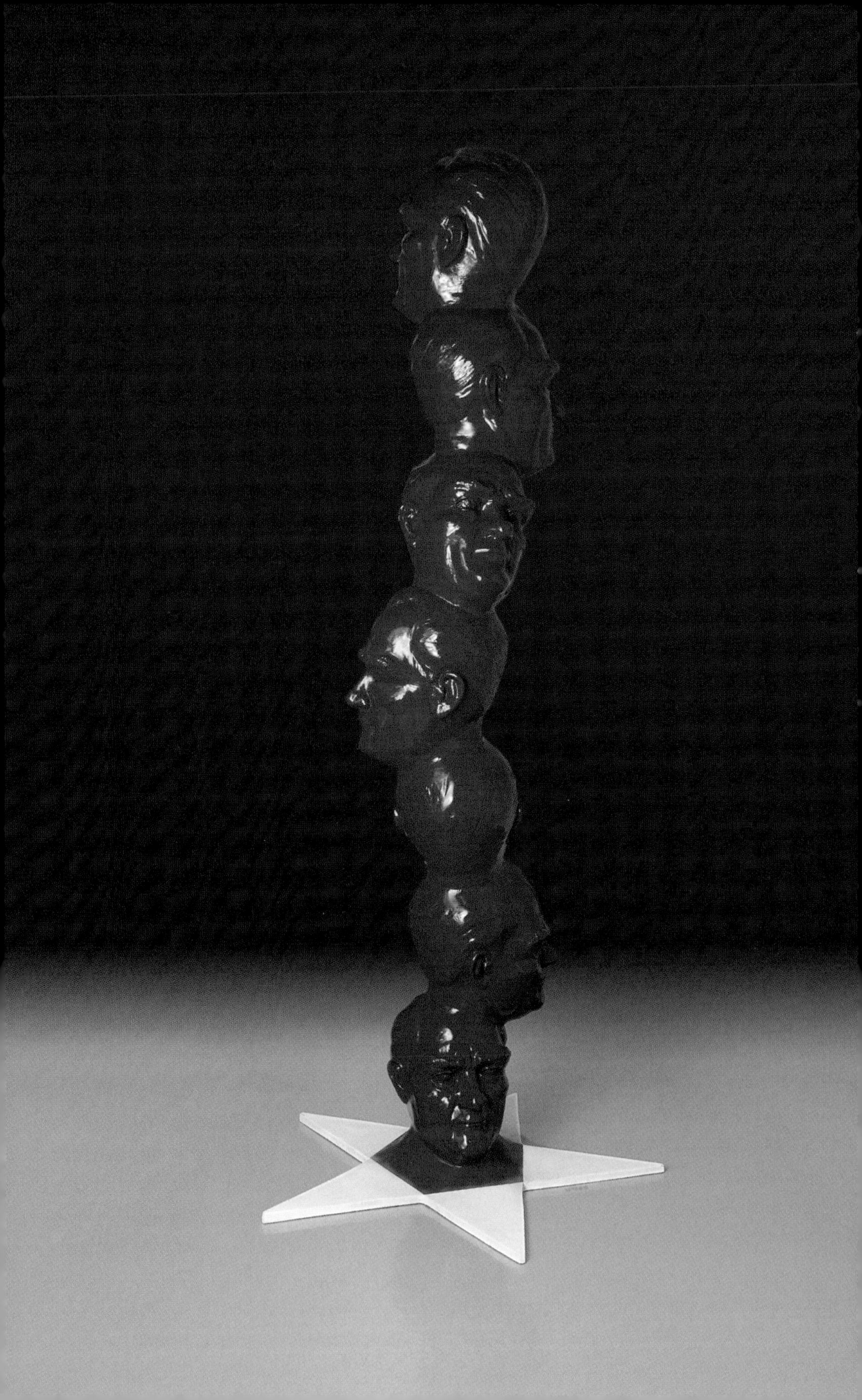

'How Do People Come Together?', mixed media on paper, 4 pieces, 30 x 42cm each, 2010. Courtesy: Nazım Hikmet Richard Dikbaş, and NON

inside. The exhibition included statues by the artist Extrastruggle, depicting Mustafa Kemal, the founder of the modern Turkish republic, as a fallen angel, complete with wings; there were equally ironic figures including a woman wearing the *chador*, adorned with satanic horns. The motivation for the attack remains unclear. Although the art world chiefly supported Demir and her gallery, some commentators reductively interpreted the incident as a miniature clash of civilisations between the traditional residents of Tophane and the hip outsiders.

On the crowded İstiklal street new spaces for art, such as SALT and ARTER, now display similar work to an increasingly international audience. Ahmet Öğüt, Cevdet Erek and Aslı Çavuşoğlu are just a few names of this new generation of artists in their 30s, experimenting with convention and the aesthetic foundations of their artistic mediums. When I ask Demir about her working methods, she tells me that she handpicks artists who all share one sensibility: sustained attention towards the seemingly ordinary; the

BOŞ ARAZİNİN ORTASINDA BİRDEN BİR SES DUYDULAR...

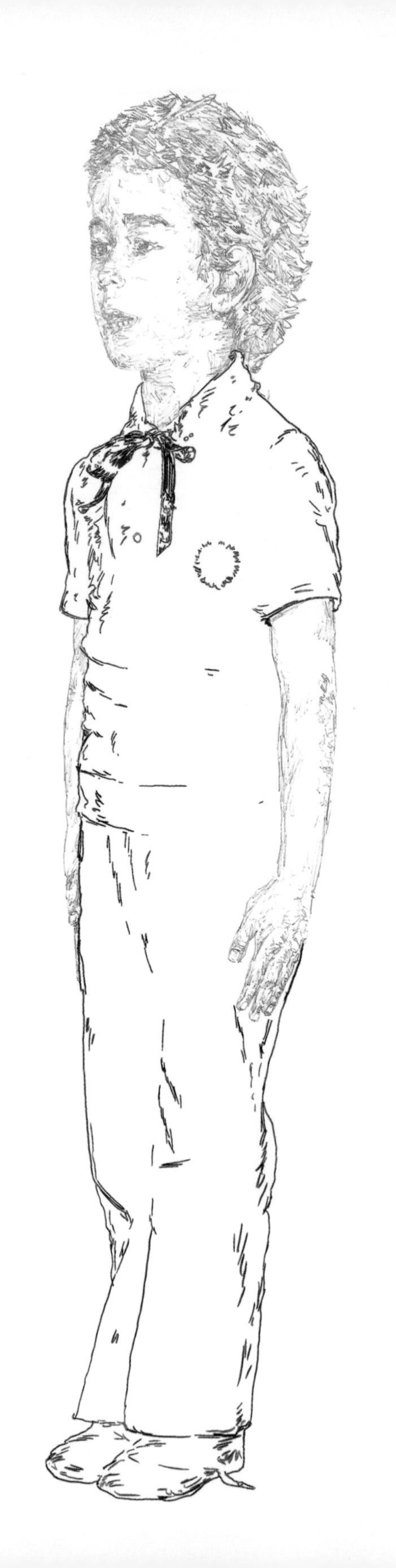

'Of course we didn't know what the future held for us', mixed media on found photograph, 7 x 8.5cm, 2011
Courtesy: Nazım Hikmet Richard Dikbaş, and NON

minor details of life. That subtle taste was evident in this year's Emel Kurhan exhibition: the Paris-educated fashion designer's embroideries, portraying penguins, crabs, owls and lions, mix the distinct realms of fashion and painting. NON's subversive, colourful, nuanced view of the world is perhaps best exemplified by the works of Nâzım Hikmet Richard Dikbaş.

Born in Leeds in 1973, Dikbaş was named for the great communist poet who spent most of his life either in prison or in exile for artistic and political activities. He began a very brief career in journalism before going to Warwick to study continental philosophy, completing his studies with a thesis on Michel Serres. His gift for drawing was only discovered almost a decade later, and for a long time he was known as a translator: his translations include Vladimir Nabokov's novel *Despair* and an excellent English translation of Orhan Pamuk's Charles Eliot Norton lectures at Harvard University. He had his first solo exhibition, *The Empire is Still Crumbling*, in 2007.

In one of his drawings entitled 'How Do People Come Together?' we see outlines of indistinct figures forming long queues, shadows drawn from different perspectives; one such queue in this four-part work imitates a real-life event where more than a hundred Kurdish politicians under political investigation waited outside court to be tried (known as the KCK trial). Next Dikbaş showed me an intimate self-portrait where the artist reveals himself reclining by a fountain, while the curiously titled 'The Spiritual Support He Sought Was Right Beside Him' portrays a man burning brightly and beautifully in red. His portraits of ordinary Turkish men and women – military figures, kitsch paintings, various characters from the working class, bureaucratic types, old and contemporary captains of industry and intellectuals – create a private, fragile portrait of a people that has been periodically muted by the state.

Dikbaş mentions a recent exhibition that brought together artists belonging to different modern movements in Turkish painting; he regrets never having had the opportunity to see a show of this nature during his teenage years. 'It gives one a great sense of security and of satisfaction. I suddenly realised that there are other people who think like me, who work with the same methods,' he says. In the 90s Dikbaş would follow other artists' work though books and catalogues while drawing his own sketches in various notebooks. 'Many of the young artists had notebooks rather than canvases, there were not many galleries around to exhibit your paintings so you would always end up drawing in and for your own notebook.'

Dikbaş reflects on the influence of the previous generation of artists, including Bedri Baykam and Mehmet Güleryüz. 'They had different political views, some artists in their generation didn't really care about politics at all. To be honest, even though I find his current politics to be a bit paranoid, I quite enjoyed Baykam's hedonistic period, that period of vagrancy; what he did back then was wonderful.' Then he muses on a sense of defeat that characterised his predecessors, resulting from a dire realisation that their secular or radical ideas were not – and perhaps in the foreseeable future would not be – widely popular in society. 'But artists are always in the minority, you need to accept that.'

His generation is sceptical of major political ideas and figures. When I discussed this with the Turkish art critic Ayşegül Sönmez, she suggested that contemporary artists aim to challenge not only the techniques and aesthetics of modern Turkish painters, but also the Enlightenment values that have historically defined them.

Dikbaş believes in the importance and urgency of revealing the political situation in Turkey 'so that it can be shown in all its nakedness. But being too explicit often results in vulgar art. One should never lose focus of the detail, of the mundane. The image does not always need to be in sharp focus to have detail; a blurry picture may also have an amazingly detailed texture.' And that seems to be a great way to describe the collective efforts of his generation – focusing on those faces and details that have long been forced out of sight. ❒

Captions

Page 139: 'A Constitution Hard As Stone', *spray paint on polyester and Turkish constitution, 55 × 72 × 170 cm, 2010.*
Courtesy: *Extrastruggle and NON*

Page 140: 'The Turkish Totem', *spray paint on polyester, 97 × 97 × 225 cm, 2010.*
Courtesy: Extrastruggle and NON

Page 141: 'The Angel Atatürk or If Rodin Were A Kemalist', *car paint on polyester, 45 × 95 × 95 cm, 2010.*
Courtesy: Extrastruggle and NON

Page 143: 'In the middle of the empty field, *they suddenly heard a sound', pencil and ink on paper, 70 × 70cm, 2011.*
Courtesy: Nazım Hikmet Richard Dikbaş, and NON

Page 144: 'Performance', *mixed media on paper, 70 × 100cm, 2011.*
Courtesy: Nazım Hikmet Richard Dikbaş, and NON

40(3): 134/147
DOI 10.1177/0306422011418164
www.indexoncensorship.org

Kaya Genç's first novel, *L'Avventura*, was published in 2009. He is a PhD candidate at the English literature department of Istanbul University and writes for Turkish and English publications

PICTURE THIS

Peter Kennard on 'Santiago Stadium' and 'Peace on Earth'

The day before my exhibition *Images Against War 1965–1985* was due to open at the Barbican Arts Centre in London on 16 July 1985, the then director of the centre, Henry Wrong, suddenly approached me and demanded that two of the works be removed. The exhibition, a retrospective of my work, was scheduled to coincide with the production of *War Plays* by Edward Bond in the Barbican's Pit Theatre. Wrong asked that the photomontages 'Santiago Stadium 1' and 'Santiago Stadium 3', both images that symbolise the bloody repression that followed the military coup led by General Pinochet in Chile 1973, be removed. It turned out that Midland Bank had hired the Barbican cinema for a meeting between high-ranking Chilean government finance officials and British bankers. To access the cinema they would have to walk past my exhibition.

The next morning, the large picture, which had proved impossible to remove in time by Barbican officials, had been covered in a moth-eaten grey blanket; the smaller one had been unscrewed from the wall. On 17 July, a Barbican spokesman told a journalist from the *Evening Standard*, 'We would hope to accommodate Peter Kennard. It's his exhibition. We don't exercise censorship.'

President Augusto Pinochet's ruling military junta remained in power in Chile until 1990.

In 1997, I was invited by the Serpentine Gallery in London to take part in a project in Kensington Gardens. Artists were asked to submit images that would then be transposed on to deck chairs. Before I had even put forward my rough ideas for the project, I received a letter from an Arts Council trainee at the gallery. I won't name her, as she was being considerate in warning me not to waste my time. Her letter reveals the usually hidden machinations of the art industry: '... having spoken with "the powers that be" at the gallery, I fear that this project may not be the best place for an overtly political artist.

'Santiago Stadium 1'
Courtesy: Peter Kennard

The indication was that "controversial" work may be at risk of censorship and I feel it would be unfair to ask you to invest in a project when this is a possible outcome.' So I was warned that I might be censored – in order to save me from the experience of being censored!

In November 2003, I was asked by Damon Albarn to produce an image symbolising the concept of 'peace on earth'. The image was to be projected on Trinity House in the City of London at Christmas. It was one of a number of projections to appear on buildings as part of the Orange Brighten Up London campaign co-organised by Bob Geldof and sponsored by the telecommunications company Orange.

I created a photomontage, using as its basis a painting of the Virgin Mary housed at the National Gallery. Partially covering her face with a famous photograph of the earth from space, I then turned her halo into a peace symbol. I sent it in to the organisers and waited. There was a deafening silence. As the day approached for the submitted works to be projected, I contacted the organisers but all I got was a series of confused messages about inexplicable problems with the image. Finally, on the day the image was meant to be launched, a slide of Nigella Lawson's mince pies was projected instead.

A slide of Nigella's mince pies was projected instead

Niamh Byrne, head of media relations at Orange, told the Guardian on 24 December that even though she found the image 'absolutely fantastic', what Orange had been looking for 'was something that people from little children to grandparents could appreciate'. She also told them that the image 'deserved to be seen' and that Orange would use it in a separate campaign to run in magazines. In a letter published in the *Guardian* on 31 December, Byrne wrote 'This is not about censorship, but purely sensitivity.'

Earlier the same year, Orange had linked up with Index on Censorship to launch the Orange/Index debates, a series of events aimed at discussing issues of free expression that took place in universities around the UK. The

'Peace on Earth'
Courtesy: Peter Kennard

Orange mission statement at the time read: 'We are ready to push boundaries and take risks, we are always open and honest; we say what we do and we do what we say: we want to make a difference to people's lives.'

The photomontage began life with the title 'Peace on Earth'. It has since become known as 'Peace on Earth, banned by Orange'. Eight years later, I am still waiting for the separate magazine campaign to be launched. ❒

40(3): 150/154
DOI 10.1177/0306422011419609
www.indexoncensorship.org

Peter Kennard is an artist and senior tutor in photography at the Royal College of Art in London. His latest book, *@earth*, produced in collaboration with Tarek Salhany, is published by Tate

KINGDOM OF THE BLIND

Writer and artist **Mustapha Benfodil**'s installation was removed from the Sharjah Biennial: Index publishes the text that caused offence

In April, Jack Persekian, the artistic director of the Sharjah Biennial in the United Arab Emirates, was fired from his position. It followed an outcry about an installation by the Algerian writer and artist Mustapha Benfodil at the Biennial. The work, subsequently removed from display, was a series of headless mannequins in football strip, their shirts covered in text, with extracts from Benfodil's own writings. This included an anguished, graphic account of a rape by Islamic militants, in a soliloquy from his play *Les Borgnes*. The drama is set in an asylum where the inmates remember the atrocities of the war of independence in the 50s and 60s and the civil war in the 90s. As Algeria prepares for the 50th anniversary of independence from France next year, Benfodil questions the extent of freedom in Algeria and asks whether a new kind of colonialism is now in place. Each character in the play is mad and tells the story of their nightmares.

In a press release, Sheikha Hoor al Qasimi, the president of Sharjah Art Foundation which runs the Biennial, said that Benfodil's installation was unsuitable for display in the public courtyard of the Sharjah heritage site: 'This work paired language that was sexually explicit with religious

'Maportaliche/Ecritures sauvages' (It has no importance/Wild Writings)
Credit: Mustapha Benfodil

DECAGE
ياكلنا الحوت أوما
ياكلناش الدود

MALIKA LEWINSKY

references in an overt and provocative manner. Like all organisations that present art in the public realm, it is the duty of the presenters of the art to work closely with the artist to determine if said work is suitable to the public context. In this case, this due diligence did not occur.'

In an interview published earlier this year on the website Artinfo, Benfodil explained that the character of Chérifa, who recounts the rape, was based on two neighbours who were kidnapped and raped by a militant Islamic group, and their family killed. 'This text isn't an attack against Allah,' explained Benfodil. 'It is an attack against the god of these people, of the Armed Islamic Group, and of other groups like them. They use the Quran to legitimise themselves, but their interpretation of it is pathological. This is what I condemn.' An extract from the play follows, along with the soliloquy of Chérifa. The characters include Farid, a young conscript in the civil war and an inmate of the asylum, Samir, a theatre director and his father, the Old Man.

Chérifa (*addressing in turn the old man, Samir, the walls, objects, the sky*): FORGIVE ME

Samir (*to the old man*): What's her story? Who is she apologising to like that? Did she kill someone?

Old Man: She was raped by 'terrorists', the warder says.

Samir: My God!

Old Man: I don't know why, when he said the word 'terrorists' I instinctively replied 'the Fellaghas'? That's what they called us – terrorists.

Chérifa:

Scratched
Molested

Mortified
Mutilated
Bitten
Devoured
Dirtied
Sullied
Defiled
GORED BY THE KORAN
Scratched
Molested
Mortified
Mutilated
Bitten
Devoured
Dirtied
Sullied
Defiled
MURDERED

Samir: Are there only survivors of the war in this asylum – or what?

Old Man: I have no idea! Leave me alone now. I need to take a nap.

Chérifa: FORGIVE ME FORGIVE ME FORGIVE ME FORGIVE ME FORGIVE ME FORGIVE ME

Farid's soliloquy: TATATATATATATA!!! HAMIIIIIIIID! Fire Hamid Fireworks Hamid hippy Hamid Hamid Boubakeur the Jim Morrison of the Aurès mountains I saw him die I saw Hamid die Die in front of my very eyes Hamid Boubekeur the Jim Arrison Jim Arrison Jim Arrison Hamid the Jim Morrison of Arris the godforsaken village where he was born he was the New Age Shawia carved from the wretchedness of the Aurès mountains his harmonica grafted onto his mouth guitar slung over his shoulders the smile of a charmer in the anus Fire Hamid firework Hamid hippy Hamid firey fury Hamid Hamid Boubakeur the Jim Morrison of the Aurès mountains I saw him die I saw you die Hamid before my eyes I saw him die and I did nothing did nothing did nothing couldn't do anything do nothing doodoo that stinks do nothing I'm scared the safety catch or I don't know what crap stopped me shouting out ALLAH AKBAR the Kalashnikov still pointed towards the ground the

'Maportaliche/Ecritures sauvages' (It has no importance/Wild Writings)
Credit: Mustapha Benfodil

extension of my arm dangling never in position because shoot a man even a bad guy it's like shooting every man it's like shooting Mankind and I left Hamid to die like a piece of music nice Hamiiiiiid it was freezing It's always cold when you're scared have you noticed guys You took out a fag like a slut and you rolled a joint right under the nose of the Rules and of the ugly death which hung off our noses and you laughed and sneered it with an intoxicated puff of fog the hashish a stimulant so you could put up with that asshole warrant officer and the horror that oozed into everything And you yelled like a crazy fool and you swore FUCKING ARMY BABY We were the masters of the poetical narcotical hazing and the Committee of Insolence was our HQ we understood fuck all about the language of these procurers of death yeehawing their fucking Rules Hamiiiiid my trousers full of holes I saw you die strangled by your guitar string the harmonica stuffed down your throat and you fucked with our guard dogs Fucking army baby Fucking army yeah! Ana omri ma nwelli militaire NEVER

NEVER NEVER YOU'LL NEVER MAKE ME A SOLDIER Light me light me light the fire that's inside me light me fucking whore joint slag light my fire We were shit scared but we were on fire every crackle the fear was so deep up our asses heady for punishment it put us in a good mood Light My Fire Kiss Me Light My Fire Light me before the War-So-Foul sets everything on fire The rusty old hourglass continued its slow progression as best it could despite the dune of dead time that had to pass through the eye of a needle The City far away sat enthroned like Cleopatra on the plinth of Liberty she was dragged from far away perched on the guard post where I was flirting with Miss Liberty waiting for the end of the world at the end of my rifle which wasn't cocked We were pissing in our mess kits we were taking the piss out of the Sharia we didn't give a fuck about the mess in the dorms we were provoking the colonels we were mocking the national anthem we were laughing at the wretched soldiers that we had become ludicrous caricatures of soldiers You remember, right, Hamid? When our superiors were preparing us for combat they didn't know whether to laugh or cry, our clumsiness was so touching, right Hamid We were like scarecrows in khaki shit brown Our instructors were desperate to make us like the others to sodomise us by uniformity As soon as we put on our fatigues the fatigues burst out laughing and our Rangers laughed at us with their open soles Even our rifles they exploded with crazy laughter, normally so serious with their badly sharpened pencil leads charged by the Universe to strew buckshot The-War-So-Vile ate it raw HAMIIIIID MY TROUSERS FULL OF HOLES They did you in made you swallow your harmonica while you were singing FUCKING ARMY BABY FUCKING ARMY OMRI Never Never NEVEEEEER you will never make me a soldier Fuck Rabbak, fuck your God, down civilian dog! Rabbak this, Rabback that Rabbak for any occasion Rabbak all the time Rabbak at point blank range Rabbak burst your eardrum and the others who replied ALLAH AKBAR ALLAH AKBAR ALLAH AKBAR they replied the warriors of Allah FUCK RABBAK ALLAH AKBAR FUCK RABBAK ALLAH AKBAR FUCK RABBAK ALLAH AKBAR FUCK YOUR GOD GOD IS GREAT FUCK YOUR GOD GOD IS GREAT FUCK YOUR GOD GOD IS GREAT we didn't know any more which god to worship I was shitting my pants I was shitting my fear my pain my cowardice diarrhoea soft balls I didn't deserve to survive Hamid Hamid was weeping all the blood from his body a hand of a strong man cut his throat without crying out watch out the wild beast is strangling him with nickel wire ripped from his guitar crying ALLAH AKBAR Hamid was lying dead holding his guitar his friend his companion his wife Your rifle is your wife screamed the captain Hamid corrected him My wife is my guitar do re mi fa sol la fuck your mother Ana omri ma n'oualli militaire

HAAAAMIIIID FUCKING ARMY BABY! FUCKING ARMY YEAH. ANA OMRI MA NWALLI MILITERE. NEVER. NEVER. YOU HEAR? NEVEEEER! YOU WILL NEVER MAKE A SNIPER OUT OF ME!

Chérifa's soliloquy:

At each rustle of leaves
At each sigh of the wind
I saw a hand pounce on my knickers
And tear my hymen five hundred times
Every night
I stood guard in front of my purity
And around my hips
I wound a strip of clay
Like a bunker of chastity
Every second
a raid of sharpened bodies
Frayed organs
Vaginas sacrificed to the phallocratic gods

My nights were haunted by all the cries of these virgins that they had
Scratched
Molested
Mortified
Mutilated
Bitten
Devoured
Dirtied
Sullied
Defiled
Scratched
Molested
Mortified
Mutilated
Bitten
Devoured
Dirtied
Sullied
Defiled
Scratched

Molested
Mortified
Mutilated
Bitten
Devoured
Dirtied
Sullied
Defiled
RAPED
GORED BY THE KORAN
MURDERED
After they had seasoned them
With the penetrating words of Allah
The sperm of His Prophets
And the saliva of his apostles
Every night
I accompanied every single one of their cries
and was petrified by their fear
and consoled by their courage
and immolated by their solitude
and killed by their terrible martyrdom
and I murmured their prayers
so that God should have pity on their souls
and take the flesh of their bodies
when they returned to the village
and the butchers spat on their fists
before scalping them once and for all
on the altar of honour
Every night
I had nightmares of a thousand penises
Erect beneath my bed
Like dreadful reptiles
That were working their way between my thighs
And were raising my legs
And were forcing themselves into my mouth
And were tearing my veins
And were bursting my vagina
With my honour and my cries
Every second

A police housing complex after a car bomb explosion, Algiers, Algeria, 1995. The explosion was part of extremists' campaign to oust the military-backed government. Credit: Abbas/Magnum

Because art is free to be impolite...

It is with a profound consternation that I heard of the summary dismissal of Mr Jack Persekian from his post as director of Sharjah Art Foundation and artistic director of the Biennial, as 'punishment' for allowing an artist invited to the Sharjah Biennial total freedom of expression. I am the artist in question. My installation titled 'Maportaliche/Ecritures sauvages' (It has no importance/Wild Writings) has been censored and removed from the Biennial.

In writing this statement, I wish to express my profound indignation after this shameful act and my solidarity with Mr Persekian and his fantastic team.

I would like to clarify matters concerning the work I presented at the Sharjah Biennial. Since the central theme of this tenth edition is betrayal, I wanted to interrogate the realm of resonance and dissonance between a writer and his society. As such, the installation works on three levels: text, sound and graffiti. The central piece is a parody of a football match involving 23 headless mannequins. The T-shirts worn by one team are printed with excerpts of my writings (novels, plays, poetry), whereas the other team's T-shirts include hybrid texts borrowed from Algerian popular culture and other urban speech forms (songs, jokes, popular poetry, recipes, board games, etc). Of course, my texts (particularly the graffiti) are not very 'polite'. In fact, the extent of social and political violence that surrounds me is as such a measure of the lack of politeness. This is what my literature feeds from.

Perhaps it is my error to have naively believed that life is not polite. And that art is free to be impolite and irreverent.

The incriminated text, 'The soliloquy of Chérifa', is a monologue from my play *Les Borgnes* (The One-Eyed), it has been performed in many countries, cities, and festivals in Paris, Marseille, Aix-en-Provence, Montreal, and in Algiers also (as part of my series Piéces détachées-Lectures sauvages/Spare Parts-Wild Reading). Some members of the audience, as well as some officials in Sharjah, have deemed the text obscene and blasphemous. The words and description may be interpreted as pornographic. This sequence is an imagined account of a young woman's rape by fanatic jihadists who belong to the sect of radical Islam that thrived in my country at the culminating point of the civil war in the 1990s. The words can be perceived as shocking because rape is shocking. All the words of the world cannot recount the atrocious suffering of a mutilated body and what is told here is unfortunately not a fiction.

The words have been interpreted as an attack against Islam. I wish to clarify that Chérifa's words refers to a phallocratic, barbarian and fundamentally liberticidal god. It is the god of the GIA, or the Armed Islamic Group, this sinister sect that raped, violated and massacred, tens of thousands of Chérifa in the name of a pathological revolutionary paradigm, supposedly inspired by the Koranic ethics. Without wanting to justify myself, I must simply underline that my own Allah has nothing to do with the devastating destructive divinities claimed by Algerian millenarian movements, the legions of barbarian beards that decimated my people with the active complicity of our security apparatus.

Finally, it is regrettable to ruin an opportunity to place freedom at the heart of the debate and deal with the future at this particularly intense juncture for Arab societies. Indeed, the curatorial team of the Sharjah Biennial highlighted the impact and pertinence of this challenge in tandem with the Arab societies' struggles for democracy. As such, I would like to pay homage to the curators, Rasha Salti, Suzanne Cotter and Haig Aivazian for their exceptional work and for trusting me.

Indeed when art meets the street and artists listen to the utterings of real life [it] is a sign of good cultural health. However those in positions of power should be more imaginative. I really hope that, in its impetuous thrust, the cycle of Arab revolutions that has shaken our tyrannical and medieval political regimes, will challenge our imaginaries [sic], tastes, aesthetic canons and thought processes. May it contribute to refresh our signs and words. The guardians of virtue ought to meditate on this beautiful Arab democratic spring and refrain from repainting the walls every time a troublemaker inscribes her or his insolent dreams.

Mustapha Benfodil
Press statement
Algiers 6 April 2011

(continued from p.163)

A mystical phallus
Gnawing ravens
A Mohammedan gang bang
an Islamic rape
A forest of a thousand beards
DRY BEARDS
DRY BEARDS
DRY BEARDS
And in each dark look
I was undressed
Then attached to a naked bed of iron
huge hairy hands
defiled with blood
tore off my veils and my nights
spread my breasts
and their dribbling lips
rolled in my entrails
and their barbed beards
scraped against my skin
and devoured my hair
Halal meat
I have been flayed right to my soul
Worn down to my skeleton
To my metaphysical membrance
And blood is flowing from everywhere.
And from every fragment of my most intimate self a bastard is born
And from every religious fantasy
An infamy
Blackout ❒

Translated by Natasha Lehrer
40(3): 155/168
DOI: 10.1177/0306422011418156
www.indexoncensorship.org

Mustapha Benfodil was born in 1968 in Relizane, West Algeria. His novels include *Archaeology of Chaos (in Love)* (Barzakh) and the award-winning *The Gossips of a Lonely Man* (Barzakh). *Les Borgnes* will be performed next January in France at L'Arc Scène Nationale, Le Creuset, before touring the country

Subscribe online and save 40%
INDEX ON CENSORSHIP
Volume 40
INDEX ON CENSORSHIP
Volume 40 Number 3 2011
Privacy IS DEAD
THE ART ISSUE

SAGE

IND
IND

EX EX

A censorship chronicle incorporating art stories from ABC, All Facebook, All Voices, Art Agenda, Art Daily, ArtInfo, Art Investment, ArtNews, *Art Newspaper*, ArtSlant, Artists Speak Out, *Ashbourne News, Telegraph*, AsiaOne, Atlantic Wire, Back of the Book, BBC, Bikya Masr, ComicsAlliance, *British Journal of Photography*, Cafe Babel, Censorship in America, *Chicago Tribune*, *Christian Science Monitor*, *Chtodelat News*, the *Copenhagen Post*, *Diplomat*, Eye on Art, Global Press Institute, Global Voices, *Guardian*, *Hindustan Times*, Huffington Post, Humanitarian News, *Hurriyet Daily News*, *Independent*, *India Times*, Iranian.com, *Jakarta Globe*, *Jakarta Post*, La Briqueterie Blog, *Los Angeles Times*, *Malta Today*, *Metro*, *Moscow Times*, MSNBC, *Nation*, NCAC Blog, *New York Times*, One News Page, *Ottawa Citizen*, Photo Lariet, Reporters sans *frontières* (RSF), Reuters, SignOnSanDiego, *Soho Journal*, *Telegraph*, *Tillsonburg News*, Today Online, *Toronto Life*, UK Indymedia, UNHCR Refworld, United Nations Information Service, View on Canadian Art, *Washington Post*, WeHo News, *Ya Libnan* and other sources, including organisations affiliated with the International Freedom of Expression Exchange (IFEX)

Argentina

For the first time in his 90 years, artist **Leon Ferrari** saw his anti-Catholic artwork displayed in a former Catholic church, the Chapelle Sainte-Anne in Arles, France, during the Arles cultural festival in July 2010. One of Ferrari's most controversial pieces, 'La Civilización Occidental y Cristiana' (Western Christian Civilisation), is a crucifix attached to an American war plane, censored in Argentina in the 1960s. In 2004, an exhibition of his work was closed in Recoleta, Buenos Aires following complaints on religious grounds from a member of the public and an ensuing court case. (Art Daily, ArtNews)

Australia

Australian artist **Van Rudd** claimed his piece on war in the Middle East was censored the Melbourne Art and Film Festival in May 2011. Festival organisers stated that the piece didn't fit in with their theme 'Inspire' and would incite racism and violence. The work depicted pop idol Justin Bieber spraying the logo of chocolate company Max Brenner on the Israeli West Bank security fence. (ABC News, Artists Speak Out)

Austria

On 22 July 2010, an exhibit displayed in the Rotunda of the Vienna International Centre was censored after Chinese UN delegates lodged a complaint. 'The Art of Peacekeeping', by Canadian artists **Sandra Bromley** and **Wallis Kendal**, featured a giant structure made from 7000 deactivated weapons, along with accompanying photo displays. The Chinese delegation complained about a picture of two Tibetan monks. The photo was removed without consultation with the artists. (All Voices, United Nations Information Service)

Azerbaijan

The Azerbaijan government was accused of censoring their own entry to the Venice Biennale in June 2011. The artwork of Moscow-based artist **Aidan Salakhova** included a replica of Islam's sacred Black Stone surrounded by a marble frame in the shape of a vagina. The president of Azerbaijan reportedly asked for several of Salakhova's pieces to be covered by a black veil because he felt they might be considered 'offensive to Islam'. (*Independent*, *Telegraph*)

Brazil

In July 2011, the controversial work *A Serbian Film* was banned from the RioFan film festival by the event's main sponsor, national bank Caixa Econômica Federal. A statement on the festival's website said organisers were given no further information behind the decision to veto the screening. The film caused controversy because of its depictions of pornography and violence. It was cut from London's FrightFest film festival in 2010 and in Spain in May 2011, the director of the Sitges Film Festival, Angel Sala, was charged with the exhibition of child pornography in connection with an adults-only screening of the film. (Global Voices Online, *New York Times, Independent)*

In September 2010, the electoral office of the attorney general ordered the 29th São Paolo Biennial to remove a photographic panel of two rival social democratic presidential candidates. Argentinean artist **Roberto Jacoby** was commissioned by the Biennial to create the piece in keeping with the theme that art is impossible to separate from politics. Election officials claimed the piece was an 'electoral offence' and regarded it as propaganda, which is forbidden in public spaces. (Art Agenda, *Chtodelat News*)

Bulgaria

An **anonymous street artist** transformed a Soviet war monument in Sofia into a colourful collection of storybook characters on 18 June 2011. Superman, Ronald McDonald, Santa Claus and Batman's arch-nemesis, the Joker, took the place of Red Army soldiers. Russian government ministers were furious and urged Bulgarian officials to punish the 'hooligans' behind the vandalism. Underneath the memorial the artist spraypainted the caption: 'In step with the times'. (*Guardian*, *Telegraph*)

Canada

The **SummerWorks Theatre Festival** in Toronto announced on 27 June 2011 that Minister James Moore's Department of Canadian Heritage had cut their funding, just a year after Prime Minister Stephen Harper's office criticised the theatre's production of *Homegrown*. The play explored the relationship between a Toronto woman and a member of a terrorist group, Toronto 18, and was deemed by Harper to be 'glorifying terrorism'. The department withdrew $45,000 (US$46,790) from SummerWorks, about 20 per cent of its budget. (Back of the Book)

Painter **Andrew Morrow** was due to show a collection of his male nudes at the Toronto Art Fair in October 2011, but the organisers informed him on 13 June 2011 that he must drape the exhibit with black curtains and display warnings to visitors about sexually explicit material. Morrow and his sponsor, Patrick Mikhail, complained that other exhibits also featured nude figures. (*Ottawa Citizen*, *Toronto Life*)

On 9 December 2010, a sculpture by **R Bruce Flowers** was covered with a cloth. The sculpture, displayed in the Tillsonburg Public Library, Ontario, featured two men embracing 'piggy-back'. The library board of directors stated they received complaints because the artwork depicted homosexual intimacy and was not family-friendly. (*Tillsonburg News*)

Artists claimed **showcase pieces** commissioned for Vancouver's 2010 Winter Olympics were removed from display or denied exhibition ahead of the games in February 2010. Uncommissioned, **unofficial artwork** expressing anti-Olympic sentiments was also removed from outside art studios in the downtown area, near the site of the Games. (*Vancouver Sun*, View on Canadian Art)

China

Ai Weiwei, designer of the 2008 Beijing Olympic stadium and an outspoken critic of government corruption, was released on bail 23 June 2011 after a three-month prison term. He was detained on 3 April 2011 and later charged with tax evasion, but has clashed with authorities on several occasions in the past. His arrest came amidst escalated government crackdowns on protesters and activists following an attempted 'Jasmine Revolution' in February 2011. Ai's associates, driver **Zhang Jinsong**, designer **Liu Zhenggang**, accountant **Hu Mingfen**, and studio assistant **Wen Tao**, also detained, were released at the same time. (*Guardian*, *New York Times*, *Washington Post*, Today Online)

On 2 June 2011, Artist **Wang Jun** was arrested for artwork that made reference to Ai Weiwei. Organisers of the **Incidental Art Festival in Beijing**, which displayed the work, were forced to dismantle the exhibition the day after it opened. Wang was released on 3 June 2011 after 17 hours of detention. He alleges that upon his release, police told him to keep a low profile. (Reuters, *New York Times*)

Artists **Huang Xiang**, **Zhui Hun** and **Cheng Li** were detained on 24 March 2011 after exhibiting pieces that alluded to the 'Jasmine Revolution' at a performance art event. **Guo Gai** was arrested for photographing the exhibit. They were charged with 'causing a disturbance'. (*Guardian*)

Cuba

From 5 June to 28 August 2011, the Museum of Latin American Art (MOLAA) in Los Angeles, California, featured the works of Cuban artists **Jeanette Chavez** and **Tania Bruguera**, both of whom have faced censorship in their native country. Their works were featured in the 'political' segment of the exhibit and addressed censorship in Cuba. (ArtSlant, Eye on Art)

Denmark

Danish art group **Surrend** expressed outrage at what they called an 'unprecedented attempt' at censorship of artistic expression. In October 2010, curators at the poster museum in Aarhus removed a piece from a retrospective exhibition that showed cartoon images of royal family members in various sexual positions. Surrend, backed by the Danish Association of Visual Artists, later published the offending poster on its website. (*Art Newspaper*, *Copenhagen Post*)

Egypt

In July 2011, around 600 filmmakers, entertainers and critics signed a petition aimed at Egypt's military council, in power since the overthrow of Hosni Mubarak in February, demanding that 'the concept of **art censorship** be reconsidered'. Sayed Khattab, the incumbent chairman of the governmental Board of Censorship, voiced his support, saying the board would approve previously rejected screenplays tackling taboo issues, such as power inheritance and the assassination of former president Anwar al Sadat. (Gulf News)

Banned graphic novel *Metro* was published in English in May 2011.

Written in 2008, the novel had been awaiting re-release after it was banned by the regime and removed from bookshelves by police. Author **Magdy el Shafee** was later convicted of 'offending public decency'. The novel deals with a variety of politically sensitive issues and contains some sexual images and content which was deemed inappropriate. (Bikya Masr, ComicsAlliance)

France

A photograph by New York artist **Andres Serrano** was vandalised on 16 April 2011 by a visitor to a gallery in Avignon. The critically acclaimed 'Piss Christ' shows a crucifix drenched in the artist's urine. It was attacked with a hammer and a screwdriver by the visitor to the Collection Lambert soon after the bishop of Avignon had demanded its removal from the gallery. Around 800 people gathered to protest on the day of the attack. Curators vowed to keep the image on display despite having to close the museum for two days. Art critics stated that the piece is a statement about the misuse of religion. (*Chicago Tribune*, *Guardian*)

In October 2010, street artist Titi plastered buildings in Amiens with anti-censorship statements and images of winged pigs and masked men. The campaign followed the closure of the **Pour Adultes Seulement** exhibition in May, when local authorities announced that the show was not worthy of public funds because some of the drawings in the exhibition were degrading to women. (*Huffington Post*, La Briqueterie Blog)

Artworks by Japanese artist **Takashi Murakami** were removed from the Palace of Versailles in September 2010. The metal, fibreglass and acrylic sculptures were said to be too 'outlandish' for the royal apartments. Protests outside the palace gates followed and 12,000 people signed a petition against the 'Disneyfication' of the palace. (AFP, *The Diplomat*)

Germany

On 9 November 2010, **11 works of art** that had been previously considered 'degenerate' were displayed at the Berlin's Neues Museum. The pieces, unearthed by builders working in the city centre earlier that year, had vanished after being seized from an exhibition in the 1930s by Hitler's regime. The pieces included 'Standing Girl' by Otto Baum, 'Dancer' by Marg Moll and the remains of a head by Otto Freundlich. (BBC, *New York Times*)

On 29 September 2010, a court ruled that the Museum Schloss Moyland would not exhibit 19 photographs taken by the late **Manfred Tischer**. The previously unpublished works documented artist Joseph Beuys's television appearance in connection with his 1964 performance piece 'Das Schweigen von Marcel Duchamp wird ueberbewertet'. The museum displayed the images a year after Tischer's death in 2009 but met with objections from the Beuys estate. It was claimed that Beuys had given permission for the photos to be taken but that the publication or display of the work was unauthorised. (Art Investment, *Art Newspaper*)

India

One of the country's most famous and controversial artists, **MF Husain,** died in London on 9 June 2011 after five years of self-imposed exile and over two decades battling against censorship. Husain's work depicting nude deities raised substantial controversy amongst conservative Hindus. During his career, galleries hosting his work were attacked and threatened, forcing curators to remove his pieces, and Husain had hundred of legal cases filed against him. In 2006, hardliners denounced him for his painting 'Mother India', which featured a nude woman kneeling on the ground creating the shape of the Indian map. India's Supreme Court eventually refused to launch criminal proceedings against him, arguing that his work was not obscene and that nudity was common in Indian iconography.

Indonesia

Nyoman Nuarta's 2007 statue 'Tiga Mojang' (Three Women) was dismantled on 19 June 2010 after the Muslim community in Bekasi, a Jakarta suburb, protested against its installation in front of a housing complex on 14 May. Protesters objected to the figures' representation of the Christian concept of the Trinity, and to the outfits worn by the figures, which they claimed were inappropriate. The mayor of Bekasi subsequently demanded the sculpture's removal because it lacked a building permit. (*Jakarta Globe*, *Jakarta Post*)

In June 2010, a **statue depicting Bima**, a Javanese puppetry character, was removed from a public space in Purwakarta, 70km south of Jakarta, after Islamic groups claimed it was offensive. Protesters claimed the depiction of a mythical character went against their beliefs. (*Jakarta Globe*)

Iran

Photographer **Hamed Saber** was released on bail on 9 August 2010 after having been arrested on 21 July for his photographs that documented the 2009 uprising. His photographs have been distributed widely in online and print publications, including the cover of *Der Spiegel*. It was the second time he had been arrested for the photographs. (CPJ, Global Voices, *India Times*, Iranian.com)

New York Times reporter Benjamin Genocchio explored **Tehran's thriving underground art scene** in April 2011 and found more than 60 museums set up in private homes. Many of the artworks were critical of the government. Most of the artists had previously been accosted by the Ministry of Islamic Culture and Guidance and had their works confiscated or censored. (*New York Times*)

One of Iran's most famous photographers, **Mehraneh Atashi**, was released from prison on 21 April 2010, having been detained since January 2010 after documenting Tehran's street protests. (*British Journal of Photography*, *New York Times*)

Lebanon

In May 2011 Lebanese authorities removed the work of photographer **Amit Sha'al** from a World Press Photo exhibit after discovering he was Israeli. His photo essay juxtaposed street scenes of past and present Israel. (*British Journal of Photography*, *Ya Libnan*)

Libya

In June 2011, after years of censorship and a dearth of protest art, graffiti expressing anti-Gaddafi sentiments was seen in several locations in Libya. The images ranged from simple caricatures to elaborate murals depicting the dictator brutalising his people. (*Guardian*)

Malaysia

In July, a court in Kuala Lumpur upheld a ban on two comic books by political cartoonist **Zulkiflee Anawar Ulhaque**. The cartoons criticise the corruption and misconduct of Prime Minister Najib Razak's administration, which authorities claim threatens public order. Also known as Zunar, the cartoonist sued the government on 20 November 2010 for banning two of his books, *Funny Malaysia* and *Perak Darul Kartun*, under the Printing and Publication Act in June 2010. He is also facing a three-year prison sentence for his latest work, *Cartoon-o-phobia*. (*Humanitarian News, RSF, UNHCR*)

Malta

On 24 July 2011, artists staged a faux funeral to symbolise the death of free expression in Malta. The funeral march followed the Malta Arts Festival, where two paintings by **Aleksandar Stankovski** were banned by the Ministry of Gozo. (*Malta Today*)

Mozambique

One of the country's most cherished painters, **Malangatana Valente Ngwenya**, died in Portugal on 5 January 2011. He was known as the father of Mozambique art and often stood up to the government in defence of younger artists whose works faced censorship. (Southern African Documentation and Co-operation Centre)

Pakistan

Lahore-based artist **Rashid Rana** admitted to self-censoring his newest exhibit, *World Series*, on 4 April 2011. He admitted he does not publicly show works in Pakistan that might cause a scandal even when there is Western interest in his work. (BBC, *Hindustan Times*)

Russia

Russian curators **Andrei Erofeev** and **Yuri Samodurov**, who staged an exhibition of censored Soviet and post-Soviet art works, were convicted of 'inciting racial hatred or enmity' on 12 July 2010. The *Forbidden Art* exhibition included works by many contemporary artists in the Russian Federation and included a controversial piece that depicted Mickey Mouse instead of Jesus Christ in a reworking of the painting *The Last Supper*. Another painting replaced the head of a crucified Jesus with the Order of Lenin medal. Erofeev and Samudurov were fined US$6,942.63 and $5,206.97 respectively. (Art Daily, Huffington Post)

In November 2010, Russian authorities arrested and physically attacked **Oleg Vorotnikov** and **Leonid Nikolayev**, two artists who participate in Voina, a radical art movement known for its bold installations and performances, which have included staging a spontaneous punk rock performance during a hearing, setting free cockroaches in a courtroom and displaying a painting of a penis on a bridge in St Petersburg. Before their arrest, they also overturned police cars in St Petersburg's Palace Square. In July 2011, a court ordered Vorotnikov's arrest for failing to meet his bail terms after he was released in February. He was also accused of attacking and insulting police during a March rally in St Petersburg. (*Independent*)

In late September 2010, several Russian artists threatened to boycott the Paris's Louvre Museum and pull their work from the forthcoming *Counterpoint: Russian Contemporary Art* exhibition because it excluded, by order of the Russian Ministry of Culture, the work of artist **Avdei Ter-Oganyan**. The artist left Russia in

1998 when criminal proceedings were brought against him after he destroyed a Russian Orthodox icon as part of a performance piece. In early October, Russian authorities agreed to allow the work to be shown, including the controversial 'Radical Abstractionism, No 8', which includes text the government claimed incited violence against Prime Minister Putin. (AFP, Artinfo, CNN, the *Moscow Times*).

Singapore

Ahead of the third Singapore Biennale in March 2011, Japanese-British artist **Simon Fujiwara**'s work 'Welcome to the Hotel Munber' was censored by the Singapore Art Museum, despite appropriate advisory notices being put up by organisers warning visitors of its sexually explicit content. The installation, which recreated a 1970s Spanish hotel bar, featured legs of suspended ham, sexually suggestive collages, pornographic magazines and and egg-splattered objects. It was closed for having been considered to be in breach of the museum's law on pornography, while the erotic magazines featured in the installation were removed without prior consultation with the artist or the Biennale's curators and directors. (Fridae.asia)

The National Arts Council slashed the budget of the **Wild Rice** art company by 35 per cent in early April 2010. Many other art groups saw their grants increased from the previous year, with traditional art companies receiving the largest boosts. A council official stated that they would not fund projects seen to be 'incompatible with the core values promoted by the government and society' or that 'disparage the government'. Wild Rice's programme included productions that celebrated alternative lifestyles and satirised government figures. This is the second time the company's budget has been reduced. (Asia One, Today Online)

Spain

A documentary about Spanish artist **Juan Francisco Casas** was removed from YouTube in April 2011 because it 'violated company policy relating to nudity and sexual content'. The film includes footage of Casas's ballpoint pen drawings, many of which feature half-naked subjects. The artist claimed that his Facebook account had been removed because of the 'pornographic' nature of his work. (Café Babel)

Syria

A **space for multimedia and performance art in Damascus**, opened in November 2010, remained open despite the clampdown on protest and freedom of expression in the country. The space, run by sisters Abir Boukhari and Nisrine Boukhari, frequently features avant garde and controversial art. (*Christian Science Monitor*)

Turkey

'Monument to Humanity' by sculptor **Mehmet Aksoy** was removed from display on 26 January 2011. The artwork, which was described by Prime Minister Recep Tayyip Erdoğan as 'freakish', depicted the friendship between Turkish and Armenian people. The sculpture had been displayed in Kars, near Turkey's border with Armenia, and plans were initiated to move it to a new location. In July 2011, two Dutch artists created an alternative version of the sculpture, a mobile art piece entitled 'Holding Hands', in the Turkish capital. (*Hurriyet Daily News*)

United Arab Emirates

Jack Persekian, director of the Sharjah Art Foundation, was fired by Sharjah ruler Sheikh Sultan Bin Mohammad al Qasimi on 6 April 2011 after exhibiting a controversial art installation that was considered blasphemous. The piece, by Algerian artist **Mustapha Benfodil**, featured mannequins wearing T-shirts that displayed sexually explicit sayings alongside religious ones. Authorities claimed that the work was not suitable for children and families and that it should be removed because it was displayed in a public courtyard. (Art Info, the *Nation*)

United Kingdom

On 8 June 2011, **Daniel Halpin**, known by his tag 'Tox', was jailed for vandalism. He gained notoriety for tagging seemingly impossible-to-reach places, and his work appeared in magazines and documentaries. Halpin has made a profit from his signature by selling tags for £75 (US$120) each, and at one point made £9,000 (US$14,424) in two hours. (*Guardian*, *Metro*)

On 1 June 2011, a church in Ashbourne removed much of the artwork from a life drawing class held on church grounds from its anniversary celebrations. Church officials claimed the **nude stills** were 'real life porn'. (*Ashbourne News Telegraph*)

On 31 March 2011, Wrexham Council refused to exhibit **Brian Jones**'s 'Brokeback Britain' print at the Wrexham Print International 2011 exhibition. The image was a spoof of the film *Brokeback Mountain* about a secret love affair between two gay cowboys. His print depicted Prime Minister David Cameron and his deputy, Nick Clegg, dressed as cowboys. The council said it had to abide with strict guidelines set by central government in the run up to an election. (BBC, One News Page)

In November 2010, officials in Hampstead, London, ordered that certain artworks at the **Gaywise Festival** be shielded from public view on the two weekday evenings and weekends when the exhibit was closed. Local authorities claimed the art would be considered offensive to the families and children who might be on the streets at those times. (UK Indymedia)

United States

Authorities removed a stained glass mosaic, 'Surfing Madonna', from the base of a train bridge in San Diego, California, on 22 June 2011. The mosaic depicted the Virgin of Guadalupe riding a surfboard. Locals called it a 'masterpiece' but city officials deemed it illegal graffiti. Artist **Mark Patterson** installed the piece on 22 April 2011 and was charged US$2,625 for its removal. (MSNBC, SignOnSanDiego)

On the first weekend of May 2011, Maine's republican governor Paul LePage ordered the removal of a large mural that hung in the state's labour department after complaints that it was 'propaganda' and 'one-sided'. The mural, by artist **Judy Taylor,** depicted historical labour events, including figures of 'Rosie the Riveter', who was an American icon for women's work in factories during World War II, child labourers and a 1937 shoe mill strike. In June, Maine's attorney general submitted a request for a summary judgment in the hope of avoiding a trial in the fight over the mural's confiscation, while lawyers for the group of plaintiffs suing LePage for denying public access to the mural filed a response opposing their request, urging federal judges to grant a trial. The project was federally funded and commissioned by the Maine Art Commission. (Huffington Post, Bangor Daily News)

On 29 April 2011, a bookstore at the Mormon-affiliated Brigham Young University removed a painting by a conservative Christian artist, **Jon McNaughton**. The piece, 'One nation under God', depicts a glowing Jesus holding the United States Constitution, surrounded by American historical figures. A university spokeswoman said the decision was business-related. McNaughton then decided to remove all of his artwork from the bookstore (Huffington Post)

Police arrested two graffiti artists featured in a 'street art' exhibit at the Los Angeles Museum of Contemporary Art. **Angel Ortiz**, known by his tag 'Laroc', was arrested in New York City on 27 April 2011. **Jason Williams**, also known as 'Revok', was arrested on 21 April 2011 while boarding a flight from Los Angeles to Ireland, where he had been hired to paint a mural. Travel violated the terms of his probation from a previous vandalism conviction. (*Guardian*, *LA Times*)

Facebook pulled the account of New York art curator **Savannah Spirit** on 7 February 2011, the day she put up photos for her erotic art show 'Hotter Than July: A Sexploration'. Facebook deemed the work sexually explicit. (All Facebook, Censorship in America, *Soho Journal*)

On 27 January 2011, the West Hollywood Arts and Cultural Affairs Commission refused to sponsor the **Tom of Finland Erotic Art Festival**, which featured gay erotic art. The commission considered the event 'in bad taste' and inappropriate for display in a public park frequented by families and children. (WeHo News, Edge San Diego)

In preparation for the *Art in the Streets* exhibit at the Los Angeles Museum of Contemporary Art in April 2011, new director Jeffrey Deitch commissioned an Italian graffiti artist, known by the pseudonym **Blu**, to paint a mural on the north wall of the Geffen building. In December 2010, Deitch asked the mural to be whitewashed halfway through its completion because of its depiction of military coffins wrapped in dollar bills instead of American flags. The exhibit was said to be 'insensitively' close to the Veterans Affairs building and the Go for Broke monument commemorating Japanese-American soldiers. (*Guardian, LA Times*)

On 3 December 2010, the Smithsonian's National Portrait Gallery withdrew 'A Fire in My Belly', a controversial video depicting ants crawling over a crucifix created by artist **David Wojnarowicz** in 1986–7. The piece was part of the first national exhibit on sexual orientation and identity. The art gallery pulled the piece after pressure from conservative groups which accused the work of 'hate speech' and a Republican congressman attacked the museum for wasting taxpayer money. The exhibit itself was privately funded. The piece was later featured in the makeshift Museum of Censored Art, housed in a trailer parked in front of the portrait gallery. (American Civil Liberties Union, Art Info, *Economist*).

On 25 May 2011, creators **Mike Blasenstein** and **Michael Dax Iacovone** received the John Phillip Immroth Memorial Award for intellectual freedom from the American Library Association, one of the best-known anti-censorship organisations in the country. (ABC, Atlantic Wire, *Washington Post*)

Brigham Young University (BYU) removed an exhibition of the work of photography student **J Michael Wiltbank** in early December 2010. His exhibit juxtaposed BYU students who openly admitted their homosexuality with a student who supported them. Following protests, the school later reinstalled the works and claimed the initial removal was 'a misunderstanding'. (Photo Lariet)

Savannah College of Art and Design removed a photograph of a sitting male nude holding and partially covering his genitals from the *Open Studio* Exhibition in October 2010. The piece was created by fourth-year student **Nicole Craine**. College administrators said that the content would be 'unacceptable' for a 'family event'. (Atlanta Connector, NCAC Blog)

Zimbabwe

On 27 March 2010, one day after the opening of an exhibition which was intended to depict the horror of the genocide in the Matabeleland and Midlands province, artist **Owen Maseko** was arrested and detained by police. Police arrived at the Bulawayo National Art Gallery and covered Maseko's work with newspapers before arresting him on charges of 'inciting violence' and undermining Mugabe's name and demeaning his tribe, the Shonas. Works in the exhibition combined graffiti and 3-D installations of blood-red paint. Maseko claimed the work told the story of a 'decade of horror.' (Global Press Institute, *Guardian*)

Compiled by Rebecca Chao and Sarah Cox

DOI: 10.1177/0306422011418293